Max
Weber
and the
Destiny
of Reason

Max Weber
and the
Destiny
of Reason

FRANCO FERRAROTTI

Translated by *JOHN FRASER*

M. E. Sharpe, INC. ARMONK, NEW YORK LONDON

This book is a translation of *Max Weber e il destino ragione*, second edition,
published in Italy in 1968 by Editori Laterza (first edition 1965). © 1968 by
Editori Laterza, Bari.

Published simultaneously as *International Journal of Sociology*, vol. XII,
no. 1 (Spring 1982).

Library of Congress Cataloging in Publication Data

Ferrarotti, Franco.
    Max Weber and the destiny of reason.

    Translation of: Max Weber e il destino della ragione. 2nd ed.
    Includes bibliographical references.
    1. Weber, Max, 1864-1920. 2. Sociology. 3. Rationalism.
I. Fraser, John, 1939-   II. Title.
HM22.G3W43313   1982   301'.092'4   80-5457
ISBN 0-87332-170-7   AACR2

Contents

Preface

I dedicate this book to the memory of Cesare Pavese and that of
Felice Balbo, to discharge a debt. In 1946 it was Pavese who gave
me Thorstein Veblen's The Theory of the Leisure Class so that I
could work on the Italian translation (after Vittorio Foa and Antonio
Giolitti had declined). The translation was published by Einaudi
early in 1949, and immediately Benedetto Croce's attack appeared
in the Corriere della Sera of January 15. Naturally, there was a
polemical exchange in Critica economica and other journals, and
Pavese persuaded me to participate with two articles in the Rivista
di filosofia. Nevertheless, the arguments and polemics of late
idealism had already ceased to be of interest to me.

I had other things to think about, for Pavese, with a certain
amount of unconscious cruelty, seemed to amuse himself by getting
me worked up. From the time of our walks in the hills of Serra-
lunga di Crea, in Monferrato, in the last years of the war (when we
amazed the German soldiers on patrol by reading at the tops of our
voices the "Chorus mysticus" from Faust: "Alles Vergängliche
— ist nur ein Gleichnis...Das Ewig-Weibliche — zieht uns hinan"),
questions of sociology, cultural anthropology, and social psychology
became part of our standard hiking gear. We were two inspired
discoverers of new sciences.

The breadth of Pavese's knowledge and interests fascinated me.
Besides the "comfortable" or "easy" class, as we later decided to
translate Veblen's "leisure class," we talked about Frazer's
"golden bough," Reik's studies of ritual, Marx and Weber, and the
fragility of human rationality and the meaning of myth as the
dawning of consciousness. Later Pavese persuaded me to translate
the psychoanalytical interpretations of the rites of primitive peoples put forward by Theodor Reik, Freud's great disciple and "re-
former." In August 1948, when I was in England, he wrote about

this jokingly to me: "And how's Reik? Have you stuck with him, or are you waiting for it to be done by parthenogenesis?" He added: "I am pleased that you're almost settled — and at Hastings too, like William the Conqueror.... I admire your courage, but clearly I am too old to do the same. I prefer to know England from books. I believe it's useful.... Enjoy the big ankles. A girl's the best way of learning a language."

Pavese was not a boy who had never grown up or who grew up only belatedly and turned out badly. He was just a peasant from the Langhe, moved to town but never completely "inserted" in the big city, always in acute discomfort in his relations with his fellow citizens, their ease of manner, and their indifference to place and to the countryside. Like any peasant, he traveled unwillingly, holding it to be a useless waste. As he used to say, "We have China beneath our feet." He was taciturn, difficult, and could also seem shy, with his angular face and his mouth set partly like a teacher's, partly in irony. Yet he was one of the most open and candid men I have ever met, someone who, after hours of silence, could suddenly become jovial and chat, ready to drain the Barbera supply of one of the wine shops on the outskirts of Turin, where the main roads end and the fields begin (or used to).

Between us there was an unconscious bond of complicity. Peasants fall into two categories: they either serve, or burn, castles. But in either case they conspire, and sniff each other out. When Einaudi's administration fell behind in paying me for my translation, Pavese went on strike. This was announced in a few dry phrases in a note pinned on his study door. Balbo couldn't stop laughing at it. But Balbo, who understood everything, could not understand, man of the city as he was, our tacit agreement.

I have already had the opportunity of describing elsewhere my dialogue with Felice Balbo — a very intense one, almost uninterrupted, which lasted from a spring morning in 1945, in Corso Umberto in Turin, to a last meeting in the Fatebenfratelli Hospital in the calm of the Isola Tiberina in Rome. Even after long separations — for my incurable nomadic habits took me far afield — we resumed the conversation again precisely at the point where we had left off. We rapidly reconstructed the main lines of the argument and sometimes finished off an illustrative example as if we had parted only the previous evening. I am reminded of Plato's Phaedrus: the only possibility the eye has of seeing itself and recognizing itself is in reflection, in a friendly eye. Between us there were many basic differences, even serious ones, in addition to the gap of a generation, and perhaps different origins and futures. Yet I cannot remember Balbo without feeling deeply the condition of fantastic, almost euphoric, receptiveness in our conversations, and also a condition of physical well-being, probably the consequence of a peaceful tension, not a competitive one, in a mutual, patient exploration.

I cannot think of Felice Balbo without remembering first not his explicit philosophical thought or his work experience, both editorial and commercial, or his political militancy, but rather certain of his human qualities that are nowadays very rare and certain attitudes that filled out his personality with a wonderful balance — his ability to listen, his openness to others and to things alien, and his attitude of happy, almost childish surprise in the face of new experience.

I remember the visit he paid us in Paris one autumn evening in 1958, when he was returning from England. We had just provisionally settled ourselves — my wife, my children, and myself — on the hill at Suresnes, not far from the Bois de Boulogne, in a little house lost in a big, rather sad, abandoned park. It looked out on the imposing, ugly grey Hôpital Foch and had behind it the unreally geometrical war cemetery of Mont Valérien (during the Resistance, Gabriel Péri died here after being tortured by the Nazis). I had decided on our move unexpectedly. In three days we had left Rome, bag and baggage, and settled in as best we could in the outskirts of Paris, on the Rue du Calvaire, Suresnes. This happened when I was sure that Adriano Olivetti had neither the intention nor the capacity to resist the "dynastic groups," as I called them then, that were preparing to eliminate the organizational structures of the Comunità movement, or at least reduce them to an instrument solely for the manipulation of workers. Felice Balbo came to Suresnes one dark evening to look us up, carefully climbing the awkward path that led to our house.

It was a peaceful and unforgettable occasion. Balbo's enthusiasm was contagious. He sat upright against the back of the chair as he talked and told stories, enunciating clearly so that the children too could follow him perfectly. He told us about England. It had been his first visit there. He was very "impressed" by it. English architecture — all those single-family houses, with their front windows — had struck him as the perfect marriage of private and public aspects, of family and society. Then came a very acute observation: the English, unlike Americans or Italians, for example, did not work hurriedly, but rather slowly and constantly. They had a better staying quality; they went slowly, but continually; they had not yet discovered idleness. Then, there was tradition. The English were traditionalists. Happy, even a bit crazy, all of them. With such a solid tradition, they could certainly allow themselves an extra pinch of madness, of eccentricity.

He told us about this with great refinement and openness. Then he spoke to me in the Turin dialect, just a few words to make me feel I was once more under the arcades of Via Po or Piazza San Carlo. I answered with some difficulty. I am not a genuine Torinese. I come from the Bassa Vercellese, and am from Turin by adoption — or perhaps not even that (with the passage of time has come adoption upon adoption, but then it is worth adopting the world).

Balbo encouraged us. He was immediately aware of our difficult material and psychological situation, and restored our morale with a perfect imitation of Lora Totino or Pella or some other character. In the house there was no furniture other than the essentials. I had set up my books in whiskey cases stacked vertically against the walls. He looked at them and said, with a quick gesture at once malicious and tender, as though he were drawing a seashell in the air, "It reminds me of Mondrian. It would make an architect think of a new kind of shelf. . . ."

It is hard, perhaps impossible, to penetrate and understand the secret of a life. Yet this capacity for listening, an exception in a world that identifies happiness with self-affirmation and has forgotten the virtue of sacrifice, seems to me one of the keys to the understanding of the destiny and the contribution of Felice Balbo. I could also add to this humility (a quality to which he dedicates a whole chapter in his Idee per una filosofia dello sviluppo umano). However, I do not wish to be misunderstood. Balbo's ability to listen was only the premise, the existential and philosophical precondition, for a dialogue in which there was nothing less than rigor, nothing indulgent or vulgarized (in the pejorative sense in which this term is commonly used).

In other words, his ability to listen not only served to indicate the philosophical refusal of monist reduction, the Hegelian possession of the Absolute, and the reflection of a recognized commonality, essential between all "participant beings." It was a generous and unyielding capacity to listen which forced others to be authentic, not to cheat. In terms of behavior, it was above all the consequence of respect for the "otherness" of others, their needs and their questions. Balbo was constantly waiting for the question,

because he realized himself in seeking the reply. Thus, his cease-
less dialogue was not only, or rather was not at all, an idiosyn-
crasy, an individual approach — it was his life. It was not a de-
vised program, but his mode of self-realization, his self—image,
his conception of the intellectual. One sees this very clearly in
an interview with him published years ago in Tempo Presente:
The intellectual is a man who rejects prefabricated truths, who
does not doze over dogmas but who poses questions and seeks replies. He continually reopens arguments that were believed closed,
closed forever.... This was a problematic consciousness, but not
problematic for its own sake; not, that is, a romantic catastrophism,
with the hybrid foundation of complacent narcissism and sado-
masochism which is natural to it. Rather, in Balbo, there was a
problematic consciousness that took on the sense of a calculated
rejection of the automatic rationality of history proposed by historicism.

Historicism... of necessity argues that the rationality of history is given and
basically automatic or even mechanical. And yet the present course of human
history presses in as an objective and demanding difficulty for the historicist
philosopher. Today, in fact, it is not men but man's products, cut off from him
and turned into social machines, which determine the course of history. These
products, rather than being a means, have become a growing obstacle to the
rationality and humanity of the historical process, to which every day larger
masses of men are enslaved (Idee, pp. 34-35).

This is a basic point in the radical critique Balbo made against
historicism, and I am largely in agreement with it. Balbo wrote:

men can make their history, but only if they know and want to act according to
the laws and determinacy of human nature; otherwise, though they may accumu-
late culture, things, machines, and despite the greatest possible activism, they
suffer history (Ibid.).

Whereas Balbo talks of human nature, I speak about middling senti-
ment, or common consciousness. This is something that can be
established not through deductivist reasoning but by means of positive social research techniques. I am talking of the meaningful
human situation, of community judgment, participation, authentic
intersubjectivity. Balbo's reasoning, even though he declared that
for him Thomas Aquinas "is neither a starting nor a finishing
point," still seems to be Aristotelian—Thomist, restoring and re-
absorbing all possible experience within the large, given, cate-

gorial and ontological structures. I do not believe that man has a
nature as a table or a chair does. Man has, makes, history; he
cannot avoid it. He lives and becomes real not in a history that is
already historical, penetrated and resolved in rational thought without "residues," but in a history that is made in and for individuals
and is unpredictable; history as a responsibility for rational management, without preconstituted guarantees, a responsibility to be
permanently discharged. The only plausible definition of man is
that he is not a perfectly definable being. Hence arises the drama
of human existence: every man every moment makes a gesture
that saves or damns him. The intentionality of human action must
be continuously rediscovered and reaffirmed. Balbo declared:
"The unreasonable rationalist trust in the spontaneity of history,
in its automatic rationality, becomes clearly absurd."

In this perspective, the paradox of our time could not escape
Balbo: in the very moment when poverty is about to be conquered
and abolished (that is, when we have the technical means to defeat
it), the demand for the higher values whose satisfaction was believed to be hindered, or at least postponed, by the existence of
poverty, has diminished. The affluent society seems to present itself as a one-dimensional society that believes in development for
its own sake and sees man's task as "doing for its own sake." It
has separated production from real needs and thus condemned itself to creating imaginary needs; it has lost the models and criteria
of judgment needed rationally to listen to, and manage, itself.
Balbo remarked: "What is especially grave and exceptional in the
situation is the paradoxical historical coincidence of an extreme
need for philosophical orientation...with an increasing diminution
of the demand for such an orientation." He was aware of the complexity of the question. His books are spare sequences of notes —
they suggest an attitude typical of the brilliant amateur. In Balbo's
work there certainly are statements that should be revised and
critically qualified. In my view there are also interesting developments, particularly with reference to technique and its influence
on human coexistence, that require evaluation. There also seem
to me to be some gaps, and whole logical expositions that are insufficiently explicit. The historical information needs to be broad-
ened — Balbo's sharp intuition is no substitute for this. Balbo
asks himself:

Is it possible to undertake this research today, seeing that, given the breadth
and depth of the crisis, it will mean reopening, at least to some extent, not only

all the basic problems of philosophy normally regarded as having been resolved or overcome, but also all the basic problems of the social and historical sciences? ...I believe one must answer preeminently along the lines of the classical fable of the giants and the pygmies, and with particular emphasis. What the giants cannot see, the pygmies will because they can, and know how to, climb onto the shoulders of giants (Ibid., p. 37).

Thus Balbo decisively began a radical critique of what I have termed the "organizational myth," or the tendency to resolve the major human and social problems of our time in terms purely of organization, of know-how. This is the inevitable result of the technocratic mentality that manages the unilateral, rigid processes of planning in East and West, a mentality justified by a common belief in history as an impersonal force endowed with automatic organizing powers. The history that is here criticized at its roots is not the real history of real men, but the history of idealist historicism, whether of the right or of the left. It discounts research before doing it, and speaks in the name of the transcendental Ego in order to limit its own interest to existence not as it is, but as it is thought; the real, all reality, is equated with known, or rather thought, existence.

Balbo went from the transcendental Ego of modern philosophy to the omni-existential ego of the philosophy of being which, in total freedom of the spirit, beyond the usual Thomist schemas and those of neoscholasticism, prepared to elaborate a philosophy as activity; that is,

the elimination of the myths and fantasies of childhood; the complete experienced acceptance of history; the sense of liberty, risk, inventiveness; the sense of the division of roles and functions in work and defined responsibilities, the duty of social production;...and above all, the elimination of the concealed, but for that reason more serious, rationalism found in various forms in the scholastic tradition (Ibid., pp. 63-64).

Balbo's elimination of historicism may seem hasty, and in my view it needs a better-articulated mediation. The philosophical knowledge he maintains and advocates is an existential, that is, an historical, historically determined, knowledge. The historicism that needs destroying is the dogmatic kind that dissolves all possible human experience in itself and reduces existence to the essence of things. Yet despite our differences, which were deep, I came to feel close to Balbo's attempt at a philosophical reconstruction because of the shared conclusion of our inquiries — that scientific (rationalist) knowledge is not the only possible knowledge, and that it does not exhaust all knowledge. If taken as incorporating and absorbing all possible wisdom, scientific knowledge falls into scientism, sanctions the divorce between facts and values, and ends up by being technically perfect and humanly irrelevant.

It is a fact of common daily experience that we are tempted by the impossible. This is not just a moralistic nitimur in vetitum. It is a temptation that goes deeper and ultimately is confused with a promise of omnipotence. That is, the impossible seems within one's grasp. What science fiction imagines is reality a week or a year later. Jules Verne's fantasy does not hold back human exploits; rather, it is too conservative.

Like every temptation, the temptation of the impossible simultaneously fascinates and frightens us. Undoubtedly it is a victory, but it is also a loss, if not a condemnation. Why? I shall try to answer this very schematically. To say that the impossible now seems within one's grasp means that the impossible no longer exists. Yet the collapse of the sense of the impossible brings with it a lessening of the sense of dramatic tension and intentionality which defines the destiny of every human being. Indeed, the definition of the destiny of man, his place and meaning in the universe, cannot be given once and for all. It is a permanent endeavor, an ever-open responsibility that is presented anew to everyone each day.

I have already stated that every man every moment makes a gesture, determines on a choice that saves or damns him. Therefore, to speak of a human nature in the dogmatic sense is profoundly contradictory. The moment one declares that man is this or that, one denies precisely what makes him a man — his ability to place himself in a problematic, and thus not exactly predictable or constrained, relation to his surroundings. Man does not have a nature the way plants or stones do. Man is something not perfectly definable. Man has history — but what history? What does it mean to say that man is an animal who produces history? "When I scratch man," said Marx, "I discover the German." But the aphorism can also be reversed: "When I scratch the German, or the Russian, or the American, I discover the man." That is, I find in the actions of individuals and groups a common need for meaning, which I feel is not easily reducible or connectable to any fixed, deduced, or revealed model, but rather reflects — if I may be permitted a highly elliptical expression — the median consciousness of men as derived from their intersubjective dialogue in a given historical epoch. This consciousness has no fixed, dogmatic content, or enforced points of reference. The common humanity of human beings must not be sought in something given, but rather in their ability to place themselves in a meaningful relation, both as regards themselves and in their relations with the world. The humanity of the worker on the production line, who day in, day out, repeats the same movement, without being able to understand its meaning in the general economy of production, is seriously threatened; equally seriously threatened is the humanity of the militant closed off from understanding others. Thus, the basic condition for the survival and continuation of humanity is the perception of ourselves as having the possibility of making history through deciding on meaningful actions whose outcome is not initially foreseen and through nonstandardized intersubjective communication based on concrete human experience. In other words, making history means, in my judgment, to abandon the conception of history as an impersonal force. It means also to recognize in human behavior an element of indeterminacy which makes it not reducible to any formal explanatory scheme that claims to exhaust it completely, without residues.

This makes for a serious uneasiness in a period like ours, an age that believes itself to be scientific. An age is scientific precisely because it leaves nothing in darkness, eliminates the mysterious, and claims to be able to clarify everything, but does not realize that whatever is too clear is no longer clear and risks becoming humanly irrelevant, deprived of meaning. This is the frontier, and the point of contact, for scientistic positivism, historicist and panlogistic idealism, and historical materialism conceived dogmatically, that is, abstractly. When progress and development are the same, and the best becomes synonymous with the different, the meaning, and even the objective possibility, of every authentic human telos is lost. Acting humanly is made equivalent to the animal's doing for its own sake. And man — a being who produces history, inasmuch as he is capable of teleological behavior — sees himself condemned to progress, as his fate. That is, he is sentenced to pure movement (production, consumption, exchange, etc.) with no necessary connection to his aspirations and his operative needs — the only motivations that could give it meaning.

Formal rationality — as expressed in the technical correctness of the movement of a machine, repeated ad infinitum, with each movement identical to the previous — obscures and blocks the transition to substantial rationality. The recovery of control over his own means of making history, and the recapture of science through its humanization, are possible for man today only insofar as he once more expresses, individually or in a group, the consciousness of his own ends, affirming their absolute and noninstrumentalizable priority. The instrument of that awareness is culture. But what culture? Traditionally, one speaks of the man of culture as a carefree man of leisure, and of culture as the product of an educative process, paideia (Plutarch). Thus, the cultured individual is a member of a narrow elite in a social condition of objective privilege, sustained by an economy that presupposes the existence of slaves. This traditional notion of culture, in which culture amounts to an irresponsible solo trilling, cannot help us in the present situation of mankind; rather than being a critical instrument it is a powerful element of mystification, in that it inevitably translates and reduces ethical problems to aesthetic attitudes, and objective questions to literary perorations. Nor can the notion of culture as a mere superstructure — the sounding echo of objective socioeconomic structures — be of much assistance. Culture is neither individualistic solipsism nor simple passive reflex. In reality, for human groups, culture is the irreplaceable instrument of self-consciousness and self-development; it is the means by which they grasp their own past and construct their own future. In this understanding and this construction there is nothing automatic or foreseen.

This is the meaning of the new integrated culture, at once technical and humanist. It is capable of ending the dichotomy between facts and values, or between what is correct and what is opportune. This does not just mean making engineers read Shakespeare and explaining the second law of thermodynamics to men of letters. It means concretely, objectively, enabling individuals to realize themselves, their vocations, and the reason for their coming into the world. This is always true, but it is especially true today. We are living in a human-limit situation, one in which we no longer have an automatic guarantee against the self-annihilation of humanity.

The problem of technology, or of the application of scientific-technical discoveries on a large scale, is the basic problem of our times. Although it manifests itself in different forms, it is determined by the fact that technical judgment finds its justification (the origin of its juridical validity, so to speak) in the internal verification of the mechanical correctness of its own operations. However, that judgment cannot go beyond itself, transcend itself: it creates no values, it cannot provide meaning for movement, or a direction for movement. More precisely than Heidegger's formulation,

this is but the everlasting return of the identical. Scientific, specialist, utilitarian, calculating, and functional society, seemingly
rational, loses in this way the sense of intentionality — the "why"
of its own movement — and tends to wear itself out in its own functioning. Once the function has been discharged, this is, literally,
a <u>defunct</u> society. In this sense, one can say it is floating in space;
that certainly it has objectives, goals, indices of development or
stagnation, but it has no aim beyond itself, toward which to move
and against which to measure itself. It has objectives but these
concern internal goals and cannot create even the illusion of a real
alternative. In the real sense, it is a society without opposition, a
society without a utopia.

This problem, which could also be expressed as the problem of
transition from formal to substantial reason (as in Mannheim), involves what is generally formulated in psychological terms as mass
apathy and alienation; these seem to be diffused at the same rate
as the prosperity of technically and industrially developed society.
In the situation and the context of such societies, alienation as
estrangement, as a lack of personal participation, can become
inevitable: one does not participate because there is nothing to
participate in, nothing <u>humanly significant</u>.

To clarify the specific terms of such a human situation is the
pressing, most important, task for contemporary sociology. This
task should never be forgotten or left out, for otherwise sociology
becomes mere operational technique interpreted as research, or
sterile formalism. However, the alternative implies a continuous,
rigorous, and critical review of its historical perspective. Sociologists, equipped with survey techniques that they believe to be
interchangeably useable, are generally too eager to dive into the
ocean of objectivity, never pausing to question themselves in all
conscience about the bases of their research. It is no wonder that
the results are disappointing: "I hear the noise of the mill wheel,
but I don't see the flour." One cannot always refute those many
critics of sociology in whose eyes (even if they haven't looked)
sociology borders on seeming no more than the illustration of the
obvious, or the mere reorganization of common sense.

The real treason of the intellectuals, and above all of the sociologists, is their refusal to introduce "into the problem" that which
seems obvious to conventional wisdom. My reading of Weber is
tied in to this perspective. It brings together ideas and interpretations with which I have been involved in recent years through the
activities of the Institute of Sociology at the University of Rome,

and with the collaboration of some of its members, especially Professors C. Antiochia and A. Catemario, and M. Di Giulio. More recently, I have had great benefit from discussions with Professor Kurt H. Wolff (Brandeis University) and from frequent correspondence with Professor Alfred McClung Lee (Brooklyn College, City University of New York) — a rich stimulus that would lead me to develop themes and problems mentioned here only in passing. In some ways these ideas have already drawn the attention of well-known Italian scholars such as N. Abbagnano, F. Battaglia, N. Bobbio, P. Filiasi-Carcano, F. Lombardi, P. Rossi, C. Pellizzi, P. Prini, and R. Treves.

Sociology only regained its academic citizenship in Italy a few years ago. However, a big victory is a great danger. Sociology raises expectations that it does not presently seem capable of satisfying. Moreover, it tends to be coopted by the prevailing economic interests, as a technique that by definition is instrumental. Sociologists react to their essentially uncertain practical and conceptual situation in the classical manner: they invoke professional ethics while at the same time taking refuge in the no-man's land of a rarefied neutrality that is at once obscure without being rigorous. Ex-Marxists are converted to Talcott Parsons's systematic formalism only to rediscover, in anti-American terms, the fluid and problematic nature of social facts; they then try the "great synthesis" between Parsons's "static system" and Marx's "dynamic system." To remedy such enormous confusions, it is pertinent to reread Weber.

Franco Ferrarotti
Rome, September 1964

Max
Weber
and the
Destiny
of Reason

Weber's Intent

In our day Max Weber has been "embalmed." The modern systems theorists led by Talcott Parsons and the natural law theorists alike have leveled against him the facile charge of relativism. They have cleverly smoothed off his sharp corners and downplayed his uncertainties, leaving us with what amounts to a photogenic caricature. This crude "positivization" of Weber has gone a long way, but a rereading of his texts settles certain questions with no room for doubt.

For Weber, a methodology was like a pair of shoes: if it isn't good for walking, it should be thrown out. The object and the method of investigation are inseparable. His focus is always on social essence. There is no dichotomy between analytical concepts and basic theory. The third chapter of his Wirtschaft und Gesellschaft, which sets out in a few pages the theory of power (traditional, rational or bureaucratic, and charismatic), is not simply a frame of reference. This is Weber's attempt to understand the society of his day, a Germany that had turned its back on agrarian Junkertum and had begun to industrialize, but lacked a real modern industrial ruling class — open, cosmopolitan, rational, and democratic. This was a Germany that in a few years would develop a massive industrial economy without a competent ruling group — one liberated from the ghosts of feudal darkness and ancestral myths, and capable of rationally managing its might.

Weber's methodology — that is, his reflections on his own work and his efforts to clarify conceptually precise, individual problems — has been built up into a system via a process of abstraction and formalization that severed its direct link with Weber's concrete, specific research. Naturally, this did not happen by chance. In Europe as in America, though in different and even opposing ways, the sociologist is still seeking professional solidity, to guarantee his security, social respectability, and immunity. "Value-free-dom," as Weber supposedly theorized it, is an ideal platform from that point of view. It is at once the precondition and justification of a neutrality that allows the sociologist, as a new type of profes-sional, to maintain a "clean hands policy" and avoid taking stands on controversial questions, restricting himself to a purely legal responsibility toward clients.

My argument is that this interpretation of Max Weber cannot be sustained. It blocks off the possibility of the development of an integrated science of man, and destroys the conditions essential for giving direction and meaning to research. It reduces social analy-sis to a wholly instrumental technique with no inherent justification for its own theoretico-conceptual or operational autonomy. The level of maturity of a science depends not only and not so much on its systematic character as on its operative and instrumental au-tonomy and its research projects. Weber's influence, still very strong among devotees of the social sciences, should not therefore cause us to be misled. His is an exceptionally comprehensive in-fluence, encompassing the fundamental contents of theories that explain society, as well as truly methodological problems, but it is not exempt from misinterpretation.

I have pointed out elsewhere how Weber himself must be held responsible for some misunderstandings of his work and the meth-odological and substantial positions he proposed in it.[1] This is not only because of the complex, composite nature of his work, which is little concerned to display a mechanical unity or to present the appearance of formal exposition. Rather, it is because of his work's internal uncertainties, unresolved problems, the contradic-tions between the ideographic-subjective element and the need for scientific standardization, and the dichotomy between means and ends, fact and value, of whose essential consequences Weber does not seem fully aware. These together make Weber's thought a necessary but highly ambiguous transition for the social sciences, tortuous and suggestive at the same time, hard to evaluate cor-rectly, and yet indispensable for formulating a sociological analy-sis that can be both scientifically grounded and humanly meaningful.

As is well known, Weber's work appeared for the most part in the form of essays and articles collected later, generally after his death, in volumes whose content is arranged according to a logical order it could not originally have had. Only the essays on Reli-gionssoziologie (Sociology of Religion) and the unfinished book Wirtschaft und Gesselschaft (Economy and Society) were conceived

by Weber himself as organic wholes. The volume on Wissenschaftslehre (Theory of Science) is made up of articles published in
various periodicals, especially the Archiv für Sozialwissenschaft
und Sozialpolitik, of which Weber was co-editor. As for the other
organic works and specific sociological investigations — such as
The conditions of agricultural workers in Germany east of the Elbe,
the Inquiry on natural selection, adaptation, professional choice and
social conditions of workers in large-scale industry, the international study On the financial, political and moral conditions in
journalism, and the famous analysis of The Protestant Ethic and
the Spirit of Capitalism — these methodological pieces, written
in the context of the Methodenstreit which marked an important
phase of late nineteenth century German culture, do not give us a
complete "doctrine of science." They are simply the methodological reflection of a lively commitment to research. Their importance lies in their presentation as an attempt at theoretical-conceptual elaboration and at the same time as the preliminary construction of a frame of reference that constantly refers back to
ongoing research.

Consequently, what might easily be taken for a mere erratic
fragmentariness finds its critical rigor and organic design in the
constantly renewed contact with active research, viewed not merely
as the mechanical application of interchangeable research techniques but a conscious selection of problems, and hence as a human
experience directed toward specific values.[2] Weber's rejection of
"system" is thus a conscious one. As he attacks and destroys the
idea of system with its implicit closure, Weber puts forward the
notion of an "open system." What may seem to be the raptus of a
polymath of genius, busy simultaneously with politics, economics,
historiography, religion, and so forth, in the name of an eclectic
and basically irresponsible encyclopedism, is in Weber a pains-
taking, radical attempt to ground an "understanding sociology"
(verstehende Soziologie). This would be a science aiming for the
interpretative understanding of social action, with the objective of
achieving a causal explanation of its path and its results. Conceptual categories cannot be established a priori; any relapse into
metaphysics must be avoided. Categories must spring from research as the origin of their validity, and must grow and develop
along with the research itself.

In this, one can see the unifying purpose of Weber's manifold and
varied activities, and the focal point of his experience as man and
scholar. The enormous range of his scientific interests, and his

remarkable erudition, make him a forerunner of the interdisciplin-
ary approach. Jaspers called this his "excessiveness," a kind of
illusion-free, heroic dedication which made him "suffer through"
problems, even as he asserted the need to dominate them by reason. At different times, these qualities could make him appear as
a man of action and man of politics, as an historian, or philosopher,
or pure methodologist. His disciples, particularly Karl Jaspers
and György Lukács, have themselves added to the confusion.
Among others, his wife, Marianne Weber, bent on making him the
representative figure of a whole era, also stresses the encyclopedic
aspect, which is clearly misleading.[3]

Weber is not a man of politics; or, better, if regarded as a man
of politics he must be recognized as a man of politics manqué, and
necessarily so. This is the tragic aspect of Weber's life. He had
a high degree of political sense, and understood politically what
others desire; that is, he could translate their aspirations into
plans for action. However, in a wider perspective he was aware
of the need to understand, as well as to act. This was understanding in a general sense, not immediately connected with problems
of the utilization of understanding and of specific knowledge mastered. His politics could be none other than the science of politics.
When he once tried to found a political party on the premises of his
science of politics, he had quickly to acknowledge that such a party
was impossible, that in reality it was a "utopia."[4] He could only
withdraw and resume the habits of the traditional Gelehrter, however personally repugnant, returning to his studies convinced that
"the qualities that make a man an excellent scholar and academic
teacher are not the qualities that make him a leader to give direc-
tions in practical life, or, more specifically, in politics." In fact,
it is pure accident if a teacher also possesses this quality.[5]

This is not just frankness. Weber is perfectly aware that politics
is action; not commentary, not initiative, and not scientific description. He knows it is "violence," "force," exclusivity, a faith
that excludes other loyalties, a pact with the devil. In this contrast
between ethics and politics there is a good dose of naïveté, but all
the same we must give Weber credit for a remarkable consistency.
Once he had identified the radical wickedness of the world and
politics, Weber did not take the shortcut of the "beautiful spirits";
that is, he resisted the temptation of an aesthetician's evasion or
a "thinning out" in abstract dialectical terms. As against the im-
practicable absolute ethic of principle he set up his dramatic
"ethics of responsibility," the capacity of taking decisions for

which one would pay personally, and the courage of "dirtying one's hands."[6] Why? Certainly not for a mere professional ethic. Weber knows perfectly well that the perfect functionary, once his function is discharged, is literally "defunct." Those who see in Weber basically a man of politics and a theorist of the priority of politics in a sociological key cannot comprehend the basic problem of his thought, which marks it in an original manner. This refers to the possibility of making political judgment scientific, thus corresponding to the wider problem of how it is possible to account for in rational terms, or to explain by way of relatively standardized causal or conditional explanatory schemas, human action and social behavior. This means including their "subjective," irreducible — historic — element as regards those of its aspects which are uniform and more or less recurrent, while at the same time clarifying the terms (the "cost," the objective consequences) of human choice in relation to values and its selective criteria.

Max Weber's politicization is a serious obstacle to the understanding of his thought and his efforts, which constitute the lasting reason for our interest. This is true for Lukács, who improperly politicized all Weber's work, proposing an interpretation that is a model of narrowmindedness and ideologico-doctrinaire schematicism, and is also true for other commentators.[7] It seems to me indisputable that Weber's strictly political ideas and the positions he adopted as regards specific questions of European and German politics of the time can be criticized profoundly, and that these rather crudely modify his proclaimed liberal-progressive, if not quite prosocialist, attitude. There are sociopolitical limitations, linked to his family background and the cultural environment of his youth, which he never managed to overcome.[8] However, his "nationalism," or more exactly his "national imperialism," cannot simply be reduced to that nationalism — "the last refuge of scoundrels" — which Lukács correctly believes to be typical of the philistine petty bourgeois, terrified by the imminent egalitarianism of socialism.[9] Jaspers not only convincingly revealed the limits of the anti-Wilhelmine policy which Weber had pursued for years, and his concern that "European politics should no longer be determined in Berlin," but also demonstrated that Weber was fully, sadly, aware of the deficiencies of the Prussian agrarian ruling group, which was still basically feudal, in leading Germany toward its responsibilities as a world power.[10] In fact, there had to be a rational choice between industrial society and a static agrarian world, and one that guaranteed social unity in the country in the void created between the fall of Bismarck and the dominance of the bureaucracy.[11] Weberian nationalism has none of the aggressive or pseudovictimized rhetoric characteristic of fascist nationalism. Rather, it is the expression of a civic commitment, seen as an absolute moral imperative. Jaspers commented:

Max Weber was the last genuine national German; genuine, because he represented the spirit of Baron von Stein, of Gneisenau, of Mommsen, not the will to power for one's own empire — at any price and above all others — but the will to realize a spiritual and moral existence which holds its ground by power but also places this power itself under its own conditions. Max Weber, who very early saw the tremendous danger into which the Germans came due to the course of the empire of William, knew that there is a limit which means ruin, after which the survivors continue, but in a vegetative state which is without political meaning and therefore without common greatness. Politics can exist only in freedom. [12]

Weber wanted to save the "realm of ideas." Throughout his life he was obsessed and spurred on by the imposing shadow of Marx. His research on the Protestant ethic and world religions does in fact tend specifically to support the Marxist hypothesis, to test its level of credibility, and to calculate its potential one-sidedness. What distinguishes it is a profound intellectual honesty. In his introduction to the comparative essays on Religionssoziologie, Weber wrote:

No economic ethic has ever been determined only by religion. Obviously, it contains an element of specific legitimacy, determined by geographic-economic and historical facts...however, certainly one of the determinants of economic ethics — and in fact only one of them — is the religious conditioning of the conduct of life. However, this too, naturally, exists again within given geographic, political, social and national limits, deeply influenced by economic and political elements.

Weber's attempt to provide an integrated, global explanation of social action that would escape the deficiencies of closed systemic constructs and the classical fallacy of the sociologies based on the "dominant factor," seemed to Lukács no more than a spurious, mechanistic universalism. He wrote:

Weber attempted to achieve a general knowledge of social history. We start a new science of the age of decadence: sociology. It emerges as an autonomous science, as bourgeois ideologists want to study the laws and history of social development while separating them from economics...therefore, as Max Weber was a sociologist, an economist and an historian, but produced an — acritical — "synthesis" of this sociology and this economics and this historiography, the specialist separation of these sciences had to remain intact in his head as well...here it is already obvious how the capitalist division of labor insinuates itself into the soul of the individual, and deforms it; and how it ended up by transforming a man both intellectually and morally much above the average into a philistine.[13]

What is really "obvious" in this analysis is nothing more than Lukács's arrogant inability to understand, and his application in a hurried and rather mechanical manner of criteria of judgment that in fact are extraneous to Weber's endeavor. One notes his remarkable lack of understanding of a man, a scientist who, irrespective of any evaluation of results, had the courage and intellectual rigor to set in continuous, problematic juxtaposition both theory and investigation, empirical datum and interpretive schema, beyond any specialist "disciplinary patriotism" or established assumption, so as to make his work a necessary step toward the construction of the science of man in society. For Lukács, on the other hand, Weber is and remains essentially a philosopher: "Thus, as a philosopher and follower of neo-Kantianism, he learned to give the sanction of philosophy to this separation and this methodological isolation. Philosophy was 'deepened' in him. The conviction grew that in this instance it was a matter of an 'eternal structure' of human intellect."[14] It is a fairly common misadventure for sociologists to be regarded as philosophers, but in Weber's case this involves a total misunderstanding. It is not even surprising that with the passage of time, Lukács's lack of understanding should become worse.[15]

Then too, there is a fairly common ambiguity. Even the most alert commentators on Weber seldom manage to avoid the temptation to look in Weber for what he himself, from the beginning, never tired of saying was not there.[16] The generalities he tried to establish cannot be found at the level of conceptual generalizations in the properly philosophical, or essentialist, sense. He is not interested in essences, and is not concerned — knowing in any case that it is impossible — to extract all the connotations of a particular object of enquiry. One is limited — and this, if one thinks of the mistaken ambitions of the founders of sociology, is a remarkable quality in Weber — to the construction of verifiable, or at least plausible, typologies for the systematic organization of the mass of elementary empirical data. As for the basic question regarding the essence of the objects of analysis there is no statement, and for a sociologist, there is no responsibility to make one. That question goes beyond the level of an intersubjective discussion in a scientific sense — one that has the binding character of a public procedure once its methodological postulates are accepted, and controls its correct application. The basic question, according to Weber, is decided on the grounds of personal preferences.

Thus, Merleau-Ponty is certainly correct when he states that one has to give a loose interpretation of Weber in order to be able to locate a philosophical system in him: "Such is the philosophy without dogmatism which one discerns all through Weber's studies. To go beyond this, we must interpret freely. Let us do this without imputing to Weber more than he would have wished to say."[17] Merleau-Ponty's advice has gone unheeded. Tacitly or openly, Weber has still been seen as having, or at any rate having been endowed with, a speculative tendency that is purely philosophical — as a philosopher connected with Rickert or Windelband, the so-called Bavarian, or Heidelberg school, the "philosophy of values," or with Dilthey, Kant, or Hegel, and there are even those who link him with Plato.[18]

These are wayward interpretations. Clearly, Weber did not exist outside the cultural debate of his time. Karl Jaspers wrote of him that he was "the real philosopher of the times he lived in," and also that "he did not teach a philosophy but, rather, he was a philosophy."[19] However, this cannot justify an interpretation that ends up identifying sociology with philosophy, and a philosophy "of existence," moreover.[20] Still less can this lead to thinking of Weber as a pure methodologist.[21] His intention was different. It was to ground the autonomy of sociological judgment. The time for this was certainly ripe.

In the last two decades of the nineteenth century, German culture had pursued a wide-ranging debate on the nature and function of the historical and social sciences, the Kulturwissenschaften. One of the open questions was definitely that of the autonomy of sociology. Denied the status of a science in its own right by the German historical school, sociology had first of all to define its task, research projects, and methodological tools. This problem was made more acute by the fact that English and French culture were aligned with Comte and with Spenser in the direction of the systematic, all-inclusive type of sociological research.

German culture, on the other hand, though trying to free itself from the legacy of the historical school, maintained the connection between the social sciences and historical considerations. Hence it maintained the link between the historical, descriptive approach and the nomothetic, standardizing, systematic approach. Particularly in its polemic with positivist sociology, it stressed the difference between historical and social research and the natural sciences. Thus was raised the problem of the grounds on which the social, or cultural, sciences could be regarded as objectively valid forms of knowledge — the problem of the basis and meaning of their objectivity. We know how the "Marburg school" carried to extremes the Kantian distinction between objectively valid knowledge and perceptions or experiences to be seen as merely psychic facts. Science and knowledge are reduced to their objective content, their logical validity, wholly independent of the subjective aspect by means of which they intrude into the life of an object. So, by contrast with post-Kantian idealism which saw in thinking subjectivity the only reality, the Marburg school saw the only reality as "thinkable objectivity."

Dilthey on the one hand and Windelband and Rickert on the other provided different solutions to this problem. For Dilthey, the historical, "cultural" sciences enter the area of sciences of the Spirit (Geisteswissenschaften), as distinct from the sciences of nature, both because of the difference in their sphere of enquiry and because of the different relationship between the subject of enquiry and the reality examined. In the world of nature, the reality analyzed is extraneous to man, while in the case of the historical and "cultural" sciences it is the human world itself, to which the subject belongs. On the methodological plane, the distinction between the two kinds of science is established by the antithesis between explanation and understanding, causality and intention.

Windelband and Rickert suggest a different solution by putting the problem in logical terms. Windelband distinguishes between sciences directed toward constructing a system of general laws and those directed toward defining the specificity of a given phenomenon. The theoretical distinction made by Dilthey between "nature" and "mind" loses its significance, as every phenomenon of nature or mind can be studied either by including it as a specific detail in a uniform whole or by isolating its individual characteristics. Rickert on the other hand distinguishes the areas of study of natural science and historical knowledge on the basis of the presence or absence of a "value relation," that is, of the criteria which allow historical research to consider an object as "specific."

We have briefly summarized the terms of the cultural debate in Germany at that time, since that is the world of thought in which

Weberian sociology took shape as an attempt to mediate between Dilthey's and Rickert's positions, characteristically by way of con- crete research. Rickert's influence as regards Weber has, in my view, been especially overestimated.[22] According to Jaspers, it was "Max Weber's influence which protected what was good in Rick- ert," and which "curbed his vanity."[23] However, there can be no reasonable doubt that for Weber, as for his contemporaries, the central methodological problem was that of the critical basis and validity of those sciences that did not seem easily reducible to a "physique sociale" pure and simple — to use Comte's term, which in addition, profoundly remodified, was taken over by Durkheim.[24] It should be stressed that for Weber the problem is never present in purely methodological terms. This indeed is the problem of a researcher grappling with specific, determinate phenomena to be interpreted critically, and whose interrelations must be analyzed not merely intuitively but scientifically. That is, they must be analyzed in an empirically relevant manner which can guarantee perfect intersubjective communicability and validity for everyone. It does not become the rhetoric of the pure — that is, the abstract — methodologist. Leo Strauss's surprise when he said that "Weber, who wrote thousands of pages, devoted hardly more than thirty of them to a thematic discussion of the basis of this whole position," is injudicious.[25] In Weber the critique of the remaining legacy of romanticism becomes an explicit rejection. All the work of the historical school seemed to him to be undermined by the introduc- tion of metaphysical assumptions, which do not permit objective study in that they discount the results of research before it has been undertaken in practice.

From a theoretical-conceptual, political point of view, Weber is closer to the "socialism of the chair" of Schmoller, Wagner, and Brentano, even though he clearly distinguishes his own position from theirs. The "socialists of the chair" had in fact commenced the task of throwing off not only the metaphysical assumptions of the historical school but also the latter's implicit political posi- tions. In their view, the first place must go to scientific research. Weber's methodology, on the other hand, was indeed built up in the course of concrete research and arose from a practical neces- sity, that of defining the function of social science and defining its instruments of investigation. Antoni puts it well in this regard when he says that "in a Germany divided by partisan pas- sions, questions of principle, radicalism and fanaticism, Weber's sociology was intended to be a foundation for rational discussion and thence for consensus."[26]

Weber freed his science from the task attributed to it by naive positivism — that of increasing human happiness, of being the new faith as replacement for the old revelations. It has been rightly observed that

it is not an exaggeration to place Max Weber right alongside Albert Einstein. Both came out of the great Methodenstreit and the empiriocritical corrosion of fin du siècle scientism; one showed the historical, the other the physico-natural, sciences the same escape from dogmatism in the wholly positive meaning given to the relativity of the whole product of experience. [27]

Weber's critique of the dogmas of naturalism goes to their roots. He wrote:

the so-called historical event was a segment of the totality of reality, since the principle of causality which was the presupposition of all scientific work, seemed to require the analysis of all events into generally valid "laws," and in view of the overwhelming success of the natural sciences which took this idea seriously, it appeared as if there was in general no conceivable meaning of scientific work other than the discovery of the laws of events.[28]

Weber argues that it is primarily in the natural sciences that the practical evaluative point of view was linked with the hope of reaching a monistic type of knowledge of all reality by way of general abstractions, a knowledge at once objective and rational. Insofar as German idealist philosophy "since Fichte" opposed the spread of these dogmas, Weber argued that "Among these problems we find the relationship between 'theory' and 'history,' which is still problematic in our discipline."[29]

In order to understand Weber's methodology it is useful to keep in mind the viewpoint, the "frame of reference," to use a term of his, from which he surveys reality in its historical development. Weber said:

The stream of immeasurable events flows unendingly towards eternity. The cultural problems which move men form themselves ever anew and in different colors, and the boundaries of that area in the infinite stream of concrete events which acquires meaning and significance for us, i.e. which becomes an "historical individual," are constantly subject to change.[30]

For Weber it is thus impossible to accept the ideal that the aim of the sciences of culture, as well as those of nature, can be the elaboration of a closed system of concepts in which reality can be confined in a definitive interconnectedness from which, therefore, it could also be deduced. In fact, as historical development changes, so too will the conceptual connections on whose foundations it is presented and interpreted scientifically. A closed system of the science of culture, and the definitive identification of questions and areas for investigation, would for Weber be nonsense, or at most lead to congeries of different, separate, points of view.

"Reality" is not a monolithic entity, but always appears differently and problematically. We must, says Weber, abandon the hope, and consequently the claim, in the scientific field, of understanding and defining reality in its entirety by stipulating laws and modes of development. Tendencies toward the knowledge of the general and the formation of abstract concepts or "law-like connections" have no scientific justification in the area of sciences of culture.

Culture, in Weber's terms, is not an area of study that can be defined once and for all, but rather a grouping of autonomous areas of research which, though they may be interconnected, are related in a way that changes according to the historical development of the various disciplines. Weber's dynamic conception of reality leads him to reject one of the basic, typical assumptions of positivism — that of not regarding a discipline as scientific if it does not establish laws. He, on the other hand, sees the "cultural sciences" as equally scientific as those termed "exact." Sociology itself is basically rooted in an explicit acknowledgment of "cultural sciences" as "objective" sciences of development. Raymond Aron, with his usual exactness (which nonetheless does not always protect him from crude simplifications), points out how Weber's sociology is progressively distinguished from history: "it is not distinguished as a discipline which establishes laws, or as a genuine science as popularly conceived; it is a complementary discipline, defined by another direction of man's desire for knowledge."[31]

On the other hand, Weber accepts Windelband's distinction between natural and historical sciences, in that they tend toward different kinds of explanation. The former try to enclose the diversity of phenomena into a system of general laws, while the latter are inclined toward the specificity of phenomena and their analysis within the particular process in which it originates and the relation of cause and effect which determine them. In addition, in the historical, and more generally the cultural sciences (Kulturwissenschaften), there occurs an inversion of the method of study in which, for them, nomological knowledge becomes a heuristic instrument instead of being presented as the goal of enquiry. As he said: "Laws are important and valuable in the exact natural sciences, in the measure that those sciences are universally valid. For the knowledge of historical phenomena in their concreteness, the most general laws, because they are most devoid of content are also the least valuable."[32]

However, there is a unity of the sciences resting on the general observance of the principle of causality as an instrument of knowledge. This feature is basic both to the logical structure of historical knowledge and to that of the natural sciences. Yet it takes on a different form in the two areas, as we shall see later. It is also true that both the natural and the historical sciences aim at the discovery of concrete relations and the formulation of norms, either as laws or as general concepts in which individual facts are contained. In this context, we must add to the traditional causal schema based on the causal chain the "conditional" interpretive schema, which tries to ascertain and interpret the conditions prevailing in the substantiation of the phenomenon being analyzed.

It is important to note that all the sciences involved in achieving knowledge of the modifications to which man is subject are cultural sciences, or sciences concerned with describing and interpreting the social action of individuals or groups insofar as it seems to be historically determined. Weber thus sees as impossible any "objective" treatment of cultural processes in the sense of reducing the empirical to laws. This is not because cultural or mental processes behave less "objectively" in a rational or "lawful" manner, but because knowledge of social laws is not knowledge of social reality, but rather of one of the many instruments needed for that task. Weber concludes that

knowledge of cultural events is inconceivable except on a basis of the significance which the concrete constellations of reality have for us in certain individual concrete situations.[33]

And again, restating this fundamental point, he affirms that in the chaos of the theoretically inexhaustible multiplicity of phenomena,

order is brought into this chaos only on the condition that in every case only a part of concrete reality is interesting and significant to us, because only it is related to the cultural values with which we approach reality.[34]

Hence,

from the point of view which stands firmly on the ground of methodology, the circumstance that certain <u>individual</u> components of reality are selected as objects of historical treatment is to be justified only by reference to this <u>factual</u> existence of a corresponding interest. [35]

He continues:

All the analysis of infinite reality which the finite human mind can conduct rests on the tacit assumption that only a finite portion of this reality constitutes the object of scientific investigation, and that only it is "important" in the sense of being "worthy of being known." [36]

Thus he concludes that the sciences of culture are attempting to understand the phenomena of life in terms of their cultural significance.

What exactly does he mean by "culture"? He defines it as "a finite segment of the meaningless infinity of the world process, a segment on which human beings confer meaning and significance." [37] In other words, the concept of culture is a "value" concept, and thus the exact sciences, and more generally the sciences of nature, reenter the sphere of culture. Weber is not interested in the event as such, but rather the event as it appears as an individual phenomenon, as a historical but culturally meaningful occurrence. Thus, in the last analysis he is not interested in the individual, the unrepeatable phenomenon or the historically particular in the first instance, but the collective, the repeatable, the multiple — in a word, the "typical" — which is still in its own way also individual, <u>sociologically individual</u>. In fact, Weber believed that

the social-scientific interest has its point of departure, of course, in the real, i.e., concrete, individually structured configuration of our cultural life in its universal relationships which are themselves no less individually structured, and in its development out of other social cultural conditions, which themselves are obviously likewise individually structured. [38]

Culture in Weber's sense pertains to a specific context and mode of observing empirical reality, from which it takes on meaning (<u>Sinn</u> or <u>Bedeutung</u>), or becomes culturally meaningful. Culture is thus made up of a mass of historical objects, of isolated elements within the complexity of the historically given, interconnected on the basis of reference to some value on which the task of conceptual selectivity rests. This selective process is decisive and definitive. Man has no "nature" the way a plant or a rock does. He has, and makes, a history; he lives, realizes himself, and cannot escape history. However, it is a history whose effects are indeed neither taken for granted nor predetermined. It is nothing else but the end result, an ever open and continually occurring cumulative process of human decisions, the sedimentation of the results of consciously reflected choices. Every person every moment makes a gesture which saves or damns him. This is the source of the pathos in Weber's thought. To see in it only the justification of a nonevaluative neutrality and the logical, historical premise of nihilism is a polemical interpretation that is hard to sustain.

By means of the concept of culture, or more precisely, of the culturally meaningful, one comes to the heart of Weber's intention, and has come upon the principle of value and all that implies. To Weber, all phenomena are cultural to the extent that their existence and their historical form affect our cultural interests, or arouse our "cognitive drive," directed according to "value ideas" that make a specific part of reality meaningful for us. All knowledge of reality is thus always a knowledge of specific points of view. Every historic object is so classified by virtue of a "relation to values," which corresponds to its cultural significance. There is no "purely objective" scientific analysis of cultural life, and especially of social phenomena, "independent of special and 'one-sided' viewpoints according to which — expressly or tacitly, consciously or unconsciously — they are selected, analyzed and organized for expository purposes."[39] Indeed, the determination that something is meaningful to us "is the presupposition of its becoming an object of investigation."[40]

Weber explains that there is no characteristic inherent in things themselves which can enable us, in the infinite number of causes that determine a particular phenomenon, to isolate one part of them so that it alone is taken into consideration. The "relation to values" not only makes the object of study meaningful but it is the criterion that allows us to distinguish the object itself. Weber recognizes the need for historical knowledge to refer to values. Regarding the meaning of value relations, Weber paid tribute to Heinrich Rickert's work and wrote that it was sufficient, therefore, only to note that the expression "value rapport" merely represents the philosophical interpretation of the particular science "interest" which determines the selection and formulation of the object of an empirical study.[41] He concludes that,

to be sure, without the investigator's evaluative ideas, there would be no principle of selection of subject matter and no meaningful knowledge of the concrete reality. Just as without the investigator's conviction regarding the significance of particular cultural facts, every attempt to analyze concrete reality is absolutely meaningless, so the direction of his personal belief, the refraction of values in the prism of his mind, gives direction to his work.[42]

Confronting the problem of the significance of an historical phenomenon, Weber argues that the process whereby the historian attempts to isolate the basic historical elements of an event presents us with two perspectives. The first is that after subtracting an infinity of elements, within which one could zealously isolate all eternity, one would not have made a single step towards the question of what is indeed historically essential in these details.[43] The other is that of assuming that no science in the world can, even as its ultimate ideal, set itself the goal of absolutely complete insertion into the causal chain of development. Weber concludes that every comparison in history implies that it is already completed, by way of its relation to natural meanings which, setting aside the infinity of the "general" as well as "individual" characteristics, can determine in a positive direction the aim and direction of causal imputation.[44]

Ideas about value direct the work of the researcher, and determine what will be the object of study and thus the specification of the conceptual and methodological tools he utilizes in the effective pursuit of the investigation. Their basic characteristic is their being "extraneous to any subjective question," even though this does not imply the conclusion that the products of investigation into the sciences are subjective. "Only the degree to which they interest different persons varies."[45] It is clear that the impossibility of a systematic organization of the sciences of culture also reveals the distance of Weber from Rickert's theory of method. For the latter, relationship to values serves as a base for the definitive organization of the conceptual structure of the sciences of culture. If for him, too, the relationship toward values is a principle of choice, then it is also at the same time the absolute guarantee of the validity of historical knowledge insofar as the values that operate in making the choice are universal and necessary. Relation to values in Rickert's sense thus performs a double function: to select objects relevant to historical science from a given group of facts, and to transcend the tangible universe by means of those values that all sciences accept as valid for attaining knowledge. In Weber, too, relation to values preserves these two functions; but he does not accept that the objectivity of the social or cultural sciences can be based on such a system of universal values. Weber believes that referring the empirical datum to values is no longer an unconditional guarantee, as the criteria for choice are no longer universal and necessary but are themselves the result of a choice. This means that, as against Rickert, the determination of the values that allow the cultural sciences to produce authentic knowledge, or make the empirical datum "speak" beyond its pure and immediate givenness, is no longer valid with reference to a metaphysical principle, even though the "relativistic" interpretation is overly hasty and basically superficial. That validity for Weber is fundamentally guaranteed by the specific orientation of the cognitive interest that guides the investigation, the viewpoint that defines the area. As Aron remarks, in Weber's sociology "the relation to values is a means of subjecting a cultural reality, made up of human desires, to objective study."[46]

However, it should be noted that for Weber the question cannot be regarded as closed in such a simplistic fashion. The relation to values on which sociological knowledge is based is theoretical and clearly distinguished from value judgment. It is only a principle of choice that makes it possible to isolate specific elements within the empirical datum, not a criterion that can evaluate action. In his methodology, the contrast between scientific enquiry and value judgment corresponds to that between value-relatedness and value judgment, in that relation to values is the basis for an analysis of relations between phenomena undertaken on the basis of empirical testing, not the setting-up of normative evaluation. There cannot be a system of values, even formally, as for Rickert, on the basis of which one can discover a system of sciences of culture, since the very choice of value as a leading criterion is historically conditioned, and these values are in mutual conflict. Further, from the moment when sociological knowledge is grounded on a choice by means of which the field of study is mapped out in relation to the variations in cognitive interests, it becomes impossible to determine the sphere of a discipline a priori. The criterion of closed definitions is ended, and the open, operative definition is born. If reference to values implies a choice all the same, this means it cannot provide human action with any guarantee of validity. Man decides from time to time, according to the various situations in which he functions, what values to accept or reject.

At this point it must be emphasized that for Weber there is a conflict between values — and not only between the different "spheres of value," but also within each one. Ethics, for instance, cannot claim to lay down imperatives valid for every field of action and does not even seem able to formulate a system of imperatives coherent in itself. The values according to which individuals align their own moral attitude, and the types of ethics following thereby, are manifold, and conflict is always possible within this multiplicity. Weber said that between values there were no simple alternatives but a struggle without possibilities of reconciliation,[47] and that this is because

only on the assumption of belief in the validity of values is the attempt to espouse value-judgments meaningful. However, to judge the validity of such values is a matter of faith. It may perhaps be a task for the speculative interpretation of life and the universe in quest of their meaning. But it certainly does not fall within the province of an empirical science in the sense in which it is to be practiced here.[48]

The superficiality of everyday life exists precisely because man is not, and does not want to become, aware of this mixture of hostile values. However,

the fruit of the tree of knowledge, which is distasteful to the complacent but which is, nonetheless, inescapable, consists in the insight that every single important activity and ultimately life as a whole, if it is not to be permitted to run on as an event in nature but is instead to be consciously guided, is a series of ultimate decisions through which the whole soul — as in Plato — chooses its own fate, i.e., the meaning of its activity and existence.[49]

Human choice of values on whose basis attitudes are given direction occurs between values that appear in mutual conflict, so that to select one or more values always implies the rejection of other values from different spheres, or from the same one.

By recognizing the problematic relation between values Weber does not, as it might appear, take up a relativist position, which indeed he rejects. The crudest misunderstanding which in his view the supporters of this "collision of values" are always encountering is that represented by the interpretation of this viewpoint as "relativism." Even if values are the products of the course of history, this does not provide an obligatory relation between them and the individual historical moment that produced them, and consequently eliminates any influence from a human stand on values. In my view, Weber on the contrary insists on that human choice which can modify the relation between human action and values, and that this in any event would be concerned with a "positive" relativism, so to speak.

The ideas about value which determine our action are for him objectively valid, but only for the sphere of our individuality. "Certainly, the dignity of the 'personality' lies in the fact that for it there exist values about which it organizes itself."[50]

In addition, one must at all events believe in values in order to try to formulate others beyond ourselves. · In this connection,

> the empirically demonstrable fact that these ultimate ends undergo historical changes and are debatable does not affect this distinction between empirical science and value judgments....even the knowledge of the most certain proposition of our theoretical sciences, e.g., the exact sciences or mathematics, is, like the cultivation and refinement of the conscience, a product of culture.[51]

The concept of value as Weber sees it, as a product of culture and thus relative to man, involves a completely new relation between man himself and the world of values. The latter is no longer in existence on its own account, provided with its own, unconditional validity. Rather, this is replaced by a relationship between normative criteria, which are valid insofar as they can be realized, and human action. The latter, by choosing between them, determines their validity.

What, then, is the meaning of the science based on this new relationship, which obviously presupposes both on the methodological level and in its analysis of human action, a human choice of values — on the one hand as the criteria that guide the research, and on the other as the normative criteria of attitudes? In other words, how can one achieve an "objective" knowledge, valid in the domain of the social sciences? In the latter, what is the function of the value ideas of the investigator, and how is the relation between investigator, and the object to be investigated, structured?

Sociological Objectivity

There follow questions that are central for Weber's problematic, but are widely and seriously misunderstood. What is the meaning, for him and us, of sociological objectivity? In other words, in what sense can we speak of sociology as an "objective" science? When the naive positivistic notion of objectivity as the simple existence of facts has been demolished, how may we reconcile concepts and reality? How may we avoid the danger of reification, hypostasizing the two terms, in purely formal heuristic modes of classification for the sake of convenience? How may sociological theory be distinguished from the basic theories of society? Is such a distinction tenable? In a word, what is sociology, and what is its use? Is it an impartial relationalization of every decision by eliminating any judgments concerning its merit — that is, a new instrument of power? Is it a systematic formal construct, with a tendency to closure, able to foresee and take for granted any possible human behavior that is intelligible in the system's terms — that is, non-deviant behavior? Or is it an attempt to establish the meaning of human action insofar as it is potentially endowed with intersubjective, and thus rational, validity?

Two interpretations of Weber's thought seem to me particularly worth mentioning. These assume directly antithetical positions, but nonetheless both present a characteristic failure of understanding. The first is Leo Strauss's. He devotes a long chapter in Natural Right and History to a critical analysis of Weber's position. Strauss maintains that Weber has not only failed to ground and guarantee the objectivity of social science through the methodological principle of Wertfreiheit, or value freedom, but on the contrary has contributed significantly toward depriving it of its human and social significance. Thus, that he had made it lose the significance of important problems, reducing it to erratic positions

of absolute ethical relativism. Thus the positive social function of the
social sciences was crushed and their cognitive, demystifying characteristics were repressed by their simple instrumentalization in the
service of the powerful of the age, be it by Hitler or by a leader
democratically elected and democratically inclined in his decisions.[1]

We owe the second definition to Talcott Parsons. He accused
Weber of being satisfied by occasional methodological reflections
during the living act of research, rather than formulating a complete methodological system that could validly have guided sociological study by providing it with heuristic models and specific projects.[2] At any rate, it is just this task which Parsons assigns himself, in order, as he explicitly says, to bring to fruition the work
interrupted by Weber as well as by Pareto and Durkheim.

I argue that both Strauss and Parsons are unjust to Weber. The
first does not seem to take into account the fact that the criterion
of value freedom, or nonevaluation, so strongly established by
Weber, helps him — historically — as a polemical weapon against
those university colleagues, like Treitschke, who used their position to disseminate their own convictions.[3] For Weber, the principle of nonevaluation was far from being an alibi. It was a means
of waging a hard and important battle of ideas against the enslave-
ment of social science, and especially of sociology, to ideological
doctrines and doctrinaire positions that lacked a scientific base in
any proper sense of the term.[4] As for Parsons's critique, it must
be pointed out that this reveals an even more basic misunderstanding, though we recognize its subtlety and often the unequaled acuteness of his analysis. What Parsons chastises in Weber is his very
historical merit: the fact that he clearly rejected the formulation
of abstract methodological procedures not associated with concrete
research, which might lead to a pseudosociological formalism con-
stitutionally incapable of understanding the problems of group existence in their real uniqueness, that is, their historically determined
nature.

Weber's position avoids these facile schemas. He is talking of
an objectivity that is not positivist or naturalistic, as those who
interpret nonevaluation or value freedom as absolute neutrality
seem to believe. Nor can it be reduced to the objectivity of dogmatic idealist historicism, which resolves the real, the whole real
without any residue, into thought, and ontologically hypostasizes it.
Sociological objectivity, and in general that of science, is produced
for man in reference to his need to enter into meaningful relations

with the world and other men. It is an objectivity for man himself, concretized not in a relativistic drift but, on the contrary, in taking positions in full awareness, and rationally (scientifically) testing his own potentialities in a given situation.

In particular as regards the notion of objectivity, one must never overlook the fact that this task of logical systematization primarily and as usual arises from the concrete foundation of the sciences themselves and their applied methodologies, rather than from a wholly speculative, abstract reflection. There is no intention thus to minimize or even to deny the fact that Weber sought on the theoretical and abstract level a justification for observations born in a problematic closer to the concrete investigations of the sciences themselves. However, this justification too seems to be stamped with the character of the work of the empirical scientist, rather than that of the logician or pure philosopher. The abstract considerations are never mistaken for absolute ends in themselves. Even terms or ideas that may easily bring to mind typically philosophical (especially Kantian) terms or ideas end up by losing their original meaning and content, that of abstract philosophy, and by remaining linguistic forms that acquire an empiricoscientific content. On the other hand, to consider that Weber's logical forms could already have a preconstituted, or hypostasized, content would mean clearly going aginst his conviction, reasserted to the point of exasperation, that no idea or thought — in an empiricoscientific sense, of course — could ever be put forward as true before accurate, rigorous testing or empirical verification. Besides, even after that they could never claim to contain in themselves a measure of absolute, exclusive validity. Precisely this is the whole core of Weber's methodology, insofar as it can be taken as the methodology of a science (social science). Once more, there is in this the confirmation that such logical forms, since they are never to be considered for their own sake, are rather a simple theoretical elucidation of concrete investigation.

It is well known that Weber's attitude and logical or methodological polemics have their origins in the German "juridical-historical school," the "German school of political economy," and consequently also, indirectly, in the "Marxist" school and the so-called "school of classical economics."[5] One can stress here, among other things, that close to the deutsche historische Rechtsschule were men such as Gustav Radbruch, who theorized the category of "objective possibility," and Georg Jellinek, whose close friendship with Weber was the source of many contributions and exchanges of opinion on the basic question of the "ideal type." It is thus fair to stress that a logical method of such importance involves from the beginning the field of methodology of law and not merely that of Rickert's and Windelband's or Dilthey's philosophy, of which generally Weber's thought reminds one.

Concerning the historical school of political economy, one should consult especially Weber's Roscher and Knies: The Logical Problems of Historical Economics — which must be viewed primarily, despite the many philosophical reflections and those on the history of philosophy, as a clarification of the method of the "cultural sciences," here delineated only in a polemical, and thus negative, mode, one not yet constructive and positive.[6]

We have already discussed Weber's involvement in the polemic and the clear contrast between the "historical school of political economy" and the school of "classical political economy."[7] After leaving the chair of law, in which he replaced Goldschmidt, Weber, still very young, moved to the chair of political economy in Berlin. He had to confront the polemic and take a stand, between Schmoller and Menger, between the Berlin historical school and the theoretical one of Vienna.[8] Indeed, this was a polemic concerning the methodology of all the sciences of "culture" in reference to their mutual definition and their distinction regarding the natural sciences. Weber felt himself facing two excesses: on the one hand, the overestimation of history, and on the other that of abstract theory. In this atmosphere of thought Weber's additional polemics against "historicism," "psychologism," "naturalism," "socialism" or historical materialism, and "positivism" in general, were born. At length, when he finally saw himself basically as a sociologist, all these polemics were reincorporated into that of the radical critique against "sociologism," and in the foundation of the distinction between sociology, the other social sciences, and the natural sciences.

Each "school" proceeded to a general classification of the sciences, a cosmology (globus intellectualis) in Bacon's phrase, in order to clarify critically the position of their own science in relation to the others. On the other hand, a study of the different methodologies arose then not only "inside" but also outside (that is, in a general logical-philosophical consideration of the classification of the various disciplines), especially strongly, at that time in Wilhelmine Germany, on the part of specialists in logic.

During these methodological polemics (which took the global, classic name of Methodenstreit, battle of methods) as might logically be supposed, every methodologist and scientist sought support in the abstract generalizations of pure logicians and philosophers, even while recognizing in a general sense the distance between concrete scientific, or methodological, research and pure philosophical speculation.

For Weber, this meant taking a position between these views and at the same time seeking another logical aid, or a methodological position that could guarantee and justify his sociological research. He realized that this meant first establishing at the methodological level what were "the logical function and structure of the concepts" and "what is the significance of theory and theoretical conceptualization (theoretische Begriffsbildung) for our knowledge of cultural reality?"[9] He knew that it was above all necessary to clarify in a critical sense the limits and extent of theoretical-abstract knowledge as an instrument of social science. In other words, this meant retaining the basic insight of the "classical school of economics," that related to "laws" — "the fundamental question of the significance of theory in the social sciences."[10] Further, in a typically penetrating statement: "The elementary duty of scientific self-control and the only way to avoid serious and foolish blunders requires a sharp, precise distinction between the logically comparative analysis of reality by ideal types in the logical sense and the value judgment of reality on the basis of ideals."[11]

However, the danger of formal abstract theory, he warned, lies in its frequent mistaking of the conceptual instrument for the objective of knowledge itself, that is, in the introduction into social science of a wholly naturalistic notion of law, with the inevitable result of making forms, and generalizing, exclusive propositions, absolute. These, instead of arriving at their sole objective in the field of social science, that of instilling order into a disordered reality, would end up by a priori closing social science itself in the face of the understanding and contact of concrete reality. For that reason, Weber always struggled against the spectre of "naturalism." He did this first in order not to repeat Comte's mistake of introducing the alien methodological rules of physics into the study of society and thus coming to abstract hypostatizations. Second, he wished to avoid the fallacy of reducing the study of society and its causality to a single determinant factor; that is, to fight sociologism along with the methodological, basic positions that, despite their heterogeneity, draw close to it — psychologism, dogmatic historicism, positivism, and more or less biological evolutionism.

One must therefore above all avoid the basic misunderstanding

of the "deducibility of reality from 'laws,' "[12] which logically leads
to interpretive schemas of the social process that are of a
monistic kind, basically proof against the needs of a constricted
social research and its tests of validity.

At the root of Weber's position there is the need to promote and
support the notion of "individuality" as the concept that qualifies
research in the social or cultural sciences, primarily sociology.
What then is required is the reformulation — correctly this time —
of the ill-conceived notion of the "relation between 'theoretical' and
'historical' work in the context of our discipline" (sociology), or
the relation between theoretical-conceptual frameworks (logical
instruments) and history (concrete individual reality — in this case
case, individual concrete society).

Weber thus mounted a frontal attack against any "monistic knowledge of the totality of reality in a conceptual system of metaphysical validity and mathematical form."

From that general standpoint, Weber polemized implicitly against
the father of evolutionism:

When modern biology subsumed those aspects of reality which interest us historically, i.e., in all their concreteness, under a universally valid evolutionary
principle, which at least had the appearance — but not the actuality — of em-
bracing everything essential about the subject in a scheme of universally valid
laws, this seemed to be the final twilight of all evaluative standpoints in all the
sciences. [13]

Thus what is wanted is a criticism of these "laws of general validity," or "laws of development" in order to defend individuality in
the sphere of the social sciences.

Weber's intention is nothing more than a reconciliation of the
"theoretical abstract method" and "historical-empirical" research.
In other words, as cited above, to reconcile "concept and reality."
This means that one must, as a preliminary, examine critically the
construction of "generally valid laws" and thus the ambiguity that
arises once certain a priori laws are established, consisting of a
confusion between "laws" and reality and reality with "laws." In
addition, one must oppose both idealism (or Hegelian "panlogism"),
which basically identifies the concept with reality, and naturalistic
positivism, which likewise ends in a confusion between reality and
the concept, at the methodological level. However, Weber believed
that although the "abstract theoretical method" may lead to the
same confusion of problems as positivism, nonetheless "the propo-
nents of this method recognize in a thoroughly correct way the method-

ological impossibility of supplanting the historical knowledge of
reality by the formulation of laws, or, vice versa, of constructing
'laws' in the rigorous sense through the mere juxtaposition of
historical observations." [14]

Not only from the point of view of method but also from that of
concrete "historical-empirical" research, one must maintain as
the "first, exclusive distinction" that between "theoretical abstract
method" and "historico-empirical research." In idealism this is
resolved by hypostasizing the laws themselves as the sole reality.
However, what "abstract theoretical method" does not see is the
possibility of "mediation," though it maintains a critical distinction. The "theoretical abstract" method sets itself up against historico-empirical research with an unmediated sharpness and
seemingly unsurmountably. To escape from the impasse one has
to "place in question," or critically reexamine the dogmatic faith
in, "generally valid laws," under which is subsumed — hypostati-
cally — reality, along with the monist-naturalist conception of
reality. One must, that is, rediscover in Weber the meaning of
objectivity, which can be reduced neither to that of positivism nor
simply to that of historicism.

The misunderstanding of the concept of Wertfreiheit has, traditionally for students of the social sciences, deeply compromised a
clear understanding of the idea of sociological objectivity. "Value
freedom" is never conceived, and is never to be conceived of in
Weber, as an absolute freedom, almost a "liberation" from values.
Rather, it points to the freedom of one who has achieved a clear,
effective knowledge of values and value judgments as distinct from
one another — even if, in my view, they cannot "scientistically" be
separated by means of a naturalistically dichotomous formula.
Such a person is free to "choose" responsibly any perspective or
evaluative point of view precisely because he is conscious of them
and tends also to make others aware of them. [15] However, Wertfreiheit is such only insofar as it allows the social scientist to
make use of a freedom of selection or choice (Auslese or Auswahl)
as regards any possible "relation of values" (Beziehung auf Werte,
Wertbeziehung). He argues: "A chaos of 'existential judgments'
about countless individual events would be the only result of a
serious attempt to analyze reality 'without presuppositions.' " [16]
That is, one has to be aware of the "assumptions" of the sciences of culture. The most important of these is that "a finite
part alone of the infinite variety of phenomena is significant"
and it has meaning only insofar as it "means" something for us,

for the current human condition. He continues:

Order is brought into this chaos only on the condition that in every case only a part of concrete reality is interesting and significant to us, because only it is related to the cultural values with which we approach reality. Only certain sides of the infinitely complex concrete phenomenon, namely those to which we attribute a general cultural significance — are therefore worthwhile knowing.[17]

Perhaps it is never sufficiently emphasized that neither "value" nor the "idea of value" ever lead Weber to a metaphysical level. These terms simply refer to what is valued, or to what is given credit, or to what one believes "valid" in the sphere of immediate, practical life, which obviously completely lacks reflective or critico-theoretical knowledge peculiar to science.[18] Now, since it is precisely the cultural sciences which deal with values, or, more precisely, with phenomena in which values are inevitably involved, these have the task of determining the terms of reflective or critico-genetic knowledge as regards values themselves. In Weber's view, this task can only be performed on the basis of a "relationship," that is, "a pure theoretical process of reference of what is empirical to values" (rein theoretischen Vorgang der Beziehung des Empirischen auf Werte).[19] To grasp his argument, going beyond the misunderstandings that push it back to Kantian or neo-Kantian formulas and which, given an interpretation of his objectivity as lacking evaluative properties, cannot avoid giving it a crudely naturalistic or positivistic slant, one has to bear in mind the relation of unity/distinction between values and objectivity — that is, the double function of value. This double function is (a) the value of the experience of practical life, and (b) value incorporated in the formulation of scientific propositions. To assume that practical life is the realm of value whereas science is "objective" because it is "extraneous" to values, which are replaced by "laws" or scientific "truths," would mean making experience blind, and at the same time would remove from science its essence as a human undertaking, reducing it to a gratuitous exercise, perfect and empty of meaning. In addition, Weber remarked penetratingly, "faith in science," or in other words "faith in the value of scientific truth," is not more than the product of particular cultures.[20]

There is thus no clear break, no dichotomous or problematic separation between science and life. Both have values in common. On the other hand, there is no simple "logico-historical bloc," no confusion between the analytic and the practical instance, between interpretation and action. To invoke a synthesis between life and science means risking a lapse into an illegitimate romantic position, basically uncritical, unless there is a guarantee of "distance" from the "lived," "clarity" and "distinction" as regards the object of investigation. Such an assumed synthesis risks leading to an empty totalization. "He who yearns for seeing should go to the cinema...whoever wants a sermon should go to a conventicle."[21] Distrust of "amateurism" in science and of "immediate intuition," which seems to allow one to enter immediately into things but is in reality an illusion inasmuch as it lacks the awareness of being subjective, is crucial here. In the concept of "nonevaluation" it discovers its outlet and at the same time its rigorous formulation. On that basis a responsible, fully conscious choice is possible for the real individual. That is, the individual can choose responsibility in that no "point of view" can be imposed as scientifically binding from outside, or without taking into consideration his own aims, interest, and "point of view." Far from inhibiting, Weber's "nonevaluation" contributes to individual initiative. In particular, as against current interpretations, the concept of nonevaluation cannot properly be seen as the presupposition for an essentially nihilist relativism, just as one cannot derive from it any plausible justification for the neutrality of the sociologist.[22] In Weber's terms, to be neutral means to be irrelevant, condemned to nonunderstanding, and to be absorbed into the "infinite richness" of reality.

The concept of nonevaluation in his epistemology is thus the methodological grasp that permits conscious, that is, rational, commitment.[23] It also marks, in my view, the moment of passing from a still metaphysical rationalism, abstract and deductivist, to an articulated, positive rationalism. This is based on objective or empirically determined knowledge which nonetheless knows that that which it values cannot be empirically, or scientifically (in the traditional sense), demonstrated as a value.

In this sense, Weber's concept of nonevaluation is a critical one. His service was that of putting in crisis the philosophical tradition within which rational choices sufficient for the individual in a given historical situation are no longer possible. However, for him there remained a whole series of value assumptions and criteria of evaluation that remained intact and beyond discussion, and which only an inadequately historical reading of his work can see as consciously relativized by him, or "transitorized" (freedom, justice, honesty in human relations, keeping one's word, sense of honor, the personal worth of the individual, and so on).

The probably impassable limit of Weber's thought lies in his not having made these value assumptions or criteria explicit. These not only are isolated from purely individual decisions and the everlasting, profound conflict between the various value positions on which an individual's choice rests but, more importantly, influence his decisions and ultimately guarantee their meaning and the possibility of making them. Obviously, Weber is completely aware of the systematic requirement, indeed the need, for a "conceptual system," which, he states explicitly, we can only produce in order to penetrate the occasional significant elements of reality[24]; but such a system does not go beyond the strictly methodological level. Just as Marx spoke of "alienation," "exteriorization," and "reification" as regards history, precisely because he felt himself deeply embedded in it and fully able to understand its course and master its development conceptually, so Weber was equally sure of the eternal stability of the basic value criteria of the European liberal tradition, of which he was the legitimate offspring. Thus it seemed to him wholly natural to avoid spelling them out.[25] Any other attitude would probably have seemed to him the result of a simple metaphysical deposit, or even a useless formula of exorcism. He could not know that the day after his death the monsters would be unleashed.

The Conceptual System

For Weber, a conceptual system (Gedankensystem or Gedanken-apparat) is simply an attempt "to bring order into the chaos of those facts which we have drawn into the field circumscribed by our interest."[1] To some extent it is thus an arbitrary or "subjective" construct. As such it is "critical" insofar as one does not forget its subjective nature and its instrumentality as regards the "chaos of facts," the "infinite multiplicity" of immediately given reality. Its objectivity, and hence its operative autonomy, are indeed linked with its acknowledged "subjectivity." This in turn comes to manifest itself as the differentiating element of social sciences, or sciences of culture, vis-à-vis the natural sciences. "Subjectivity," or the will — the concrete initiative of individuals who through their historical action transform reality, driven by their interests and aspirations — guides them by means of their particular "points of view." As Weber says:

The intellectual apparatus which the past has developed through the analysis, or more truthfully, the analytical rearrangement of the immediately given reality, and through the latter's integration by concepts which correspond to the state of its knowledge and the focus of its interest, is in constant tension with the new knowledge which we can and desire to wrest from reality. The progress of cultural science occurs through this conflict.[2]

The progress of the social sciences, or sciences of culture, is thus dependent on the conscious taking on of particular "points of view" on the part of the social investigator, and his "specific requests," his concrete concerns determined in relation to a reality which left to itself is amorphous and "chaotic." This must be stressed. It involves in a critical sense the two basic conceptions that dominate the field of contemporary social science and reveal its basic, methodological deficiencies: (a) the conception of the closed conceptual system, either at the middle range as in

32

Robert K. Merton,[3] or fully, as in Talcott Parsons[4]; (b) the conception of the progress of knowledge in the social sciences by way of standardization and accumulation of research findings.

In fact, these conceptions presuppose in their different ways an essentially immobile social reality which is absolutely intelligible, authoritatively valid. It is translatable, and may be fully expressed (though only gradually and with the right logical-linguistic grasp) by means of the accumulation of partial findings arrived at from time to time, in a complete conceptual system at least tendentially logically closed. It is this claim which Weber destroys. There can undoubtedly be a particular kind of accumulation in the social sciences. This concerns natural aspects and elements of social phenomena. However, this should not be taken as equivalent to the whole of the nature of social "reality," which seems on the contrary distinguished by a special type of cumulability, one that is highly problematic. This has to be critically rethought ab imis, and reassessed in every new situation by the standard of the new values — interests, aspirations, and "points of view." This cumulability is a genuine dialectical movement, by definition not a mechanical but an historical one that rejects juxtapositions and is not simply nomothetic, conventionalist, and "external."

In other words, the investigator, far from being neutral, is constantly called into question: this challenges his very being, in the center of the problem, and this gives meaning and relevance to sociological analysis. In several places Weber stresses the need for the researcher to have at his disposal points of view that are indispensable to determine what is and is not important throughout the research. However, this comes with the warning not to try to construct a complete conceptual system — not to fall victim to the presumption of thinking history before knowing it — thereby taking for granted in advance all possible outcomes of the study and thus nullifying it. To avoid any kind of scientistic misunderstanding, Weber argues: "An empirical science cannot tell anyone what he should do — but rather what he can do — and, in certain circumstances, what he wishes to do."[5] Value judgment regarding a subject means

my "taking an attitude" in a certain concrete way to the object in its concrete individuality; the subjective sources of this attitude of mine, of my "value standpoints" which are decisive for it, are definitely not a "concept," and certainly not an "abstract concept" but rather a thoroughly concrete, highly individually structured and constituted "feeling" and "preference"; it may, however, be under certain circumstances the consciousness of a certain, and here again, concrete kind of imperative (<u>sollens</u>).[6]

The basic assumption of sociological analysis and the sciences of culture is thus not that we possess a particular culture endowed with value but rather that <u>we are cultural beings</u>, capable of assuming a position vis-à-vis the world, and giving sense to it. This means that for Weber the investigator must not be a <u>tabula rasa</u> but, on the contrary, must have points of view, which are indispensable, as explained above, for distinguishing what is and is not important in a material world amorphous in itself.

By virtue of these ideas about value we isolate in the real world what is meaningful for us. Weber does not conceal the fact that in the sphere of the social sciences various "personal ways of understanding the world" come into play. However, it is not the job of an empirical science to make judgments regarding the validity of these values. Between the level of actual existence, which is rightly that of scientific enquiry, and that of ideal validity, which is properly that of value judgment, there can be no passage, since one would thus meet with arbitrary confusion. For Weber, personal values are a point of departure. Once their initial function has been discharged they must not influence or obfuscate scientific research in any way, even in the area of determining simple causal connections between facts. In his polemic with Eduard Meyer, Weber accused him of simply confusing "valuable" with "causally important."[7] It is not by chance that Weber speaks of "feeling" and "seeing" concretely. Indeed, the subject assumes a position vis-à-vis reality on the ground of the sphere of ideals — ethical, aesthetic, and religious values, ideas about value. These are always relative to the subject, and not necessarily mutually harmonious, because they are historically conditioned. Weber noted that "Endless misunderstanding and a great deal of terminological — and hence sterile — conflict have taken place about the term 'value judgment.'"[8] He continues:

What is really at issue is the intrinsically simple demand that the investigator and teacher should keep unconditionally separate the establishment of empirical facts (including the "value-oriented" conduct of the empirical individual whom he is investigating) and his own practical evaluations, i.e., his evaluation of these facts as satisfactory or unsatisfactory (including among these facts evaluations made by the empirical persons who are the objects of investigation).[9]

Independent of the content of this "position taking," the scientific interest of phenomena rests on the cultural meaning they hold for

us. Weber says that a specific practical rule, an objective established a priori, may certainly be the presupposition of discussion
and enquiry, and thus only discussion of the means for carrying it
out would be required. This is indisputable, but precisely in that
discussion of means it will become clear that the same aim is desired on very different grounds. "In other words, in what sense
can the evaluation, which the individual asserts, be treated, not as
a fact but as the object of scientific criticism?"[10]

Nothing can guarantee that the object of a particular enquiry is
worth being known, just as nothing can guarantee that the objectives
of a particular technical elaboration have an effective validity.
This holds also for the natural disciplines, for physics, chemistry,
and biology. These help us technically to master life, but the
problem of whether or not all of that has meaning must be either
assumed in their aims or completely ignored.

The same happens in the social sciences. According to Weber,
these tell us nothing about the validity of the object of their enquiry. In the same way, by itself the technical function tells us
nothing about the meaning of science. It is the result of verification as regards functional correctness, within its own operations.
As for the problem of the meaning of science for man and his place
in the universe, it is impotent and has no suggestions to offer.

Any discussion of the "worthiness" of practical evaluations, especially ethical ones, is thus for Weber out of place in the field of
science, as it "belongs among the tasks of social philosophy."[11]

He does not deny the possibility of a technical critique of value
judgments in the sphere of science, but this can lead the investigator only to "self-reflection." The social sciences can take on
values as their own object only on the factual plane, by considering
the relation between means and end implicit in their realization
and performing the task of critical analysis on an empirical basis.
"To apply the results of this analysis in the making of a decision,
however, is not a task which science can undertake."[12] The investigator will translate the "measurement" of value into decisions on
his own account, since this is certainly not the job of science but
his personal affair, concerning his will and conscience. The investigator

weighs and chooses from among the values involved according to his own conscience and his personal view of the world. Science can make him realize that
all action and naturally, according to the circumstances, inaction imply in their
consequences the espousal of certain values — and herewith — what is today so

willingly overlooked — the rejection of certain others. The act of choice itself
is his own responsibility. [13]

The objectivity of the knowledge of the social sciences, as Weber
never tired of saying, rests on the fact that "the empirical data are
always related to those evaluative ideas which alone make them
worth knowing, and the significance of the empirical data is derived
from these evaluative ideas. But these data can never become the
foundation for the empirically impossible proof of the validity of
the evaluative ideas." [14]

By this, Weber does not seem to wish to ignore the importance
of these "supreme values," which are always decisive for the direction taken each time by the ordering activity of human thought.
However, these represent only the initial stimulus for the research,
which must then proceed objectively — that is, rationally. He clar-
ifies this:

The capacity to distinguish between empirical knowledge and value judgments,
and the fulfillment of the scientific duty to see the factual truth as well as the
practical duty to stand up for our own ideals, constitute the program to which
we wish to adhere with ever increasing firmness. [15]

The scientist confronted with some particular problem in which
different values are involved cannot have recourse to science to
make his decisions. According to Weber:

In practice, you can take this or that position when concerned with a problem
of value — for simplicity's sake, please think of social phenomena as examples.
If you take such and such a stand, then, according to scientific experience, you
have to use such and such a means in order to carry out your conviction prac-
tically. Now, these means are perhaps such that you believe you must reject them.
Then you simply must choose between the end and the inevitable means. [16]

The outcome of science is thus the taking of a conscious position
in the face of human action as regards the specifying of the conditions for testing the values which give significance and sense of
direction to that action.

Thus, for Weber, political philosophy becomes the methodology
of political science, entrusted with the important function of forc-
ing or at least helping the individual to come to terms with his
own appreciation of the matter. [17] In his view, philosophy, in dis-
charging this important responsibility, also places itself at the service of ethics, since it promotes clarity and the sense of responsibility.

Weber's science is thus essentially a technical one of means and costs, so arranged, that is, as to foresee the possibilities, limits, and the inevitable consequences, even the undesired ones, of a procedure begun in the name of a specific value judgment. Research, and the conceptual system in which it is expressed, seems to be dominated by the initial, and at the same time basic, dimension of choice. Weber takes an obvious risk, that of theorizing a science that has ceased to be one, a science reduced to technique. He fends off this risk by arguing that the dualism of science value judgments does not mean that the empirical sciences should stop when faced with any type of factual evidence at all, while at the same time stressing the problematic character of science. Choice and intention: the problematic nature of Weber's methodology rests on these. As we have already pointed out, closed and hypostasized definitions of science are destroyed by them. Every science creates its own object and elaborates its own procedural rules without in any way thus returning to the metaphysical plane. Scientific procedure has its own self-justification, the criterion for evaluating its own correctness, and the possibility of an autonomous process of conceptual self-correction on the basis of empirical data methodically explored. "The specific function of science," concludes Weber, "is just the opposite: namely, to ask questions about these things which convention makes self-evident."[18]

Just as certain ethical and religious convictions cannot be maintained as "imbued with value" or shared because they are causally highly efficacious, so too with the affirmation of the value of an ethical or religious phenomenon, one does not qualify the enormous consequences its realization has had or might have. "The empirical-psychological and historical analysis of certain evaluations with respect to the individual social conditions of their emergence and continued existence can never, under any circumstances, lead to anything other than an 'understanding' explanation."[19]

Sociology does not console. It can render to politicians and parties only the "inestimable service" of telling them that "(1) these and these 'ultimate' positions are conceivable with reference to this practical problem; (2) such and such are the facts which you must take into account in making your choice between these positions."[20] It tends, that is, to demystify the taking of positions. However, the question cannot be dealt with so summarily.

There are some problems regarding Weber's distinction between "knowing" and "valuing," or judgment of the fact seen as knowledge and value judgment seen as evaluation. How can one know without evaluating, and vice versa? He seems not to grasp the dialectical link, the connection of reciprocal influence, which necessarily connects these two moments. That would explain the current interpretation of a rupture between fact and value as guarantee of the objectivity of research, and the utopian claim, grossly misleading in any case, of an absolute neutrality on the observer's part.

In other words, the question is whether we, by way of knowledge, can achieve an ethical transformation. What is sociological knowledge? Can it really be reduced to a simple question of unmotivated (or idle) curiosity, to use Veblen's formula? Weber himself seems to believe that social science is not without a specific operational efficiency when it formulates a science that, stripped of any presuppositions, can probe the depths of reality — especially its more "inconvenient" aspects. Why "inconvenient"? The use of that word cannot be fortuitous. It is probably supposed to mark a possible process of review of social reality. On the other hand, evaluation, while deriving from a function separate from that of "understanding," is only possible on the basis of science, which is the first to recognize it as its own. In fact, through them one expresses what scientific research is concerned to attain.

In a mood of neoromantic fatalism (which should be remembered in the light of contemporary efforts to "positivize" him) Weber argues that in every age there exists, and will exist, an insurmountable difference between what relates to our feelings and "ability to be enthusiastic over practical goals or cultural content," and what instead centers on our power and need to order empirical reality conceptually. He is thus aware, and periodically stresses, that without the "point of view," or the individual's ideas of value, themselves the product of a human choice, empirical reality would still be amorphous, and no science would be possible. Both object and method of research are based on human "attitudes." To recognize the dimension of choice as basic in the process of knowledge clearly involves the further problem of clarifying by what procedure it is possible to prove a cause–effect relation in its appearance in a given phenomenon.

Weber argued for the infinite multiplicity of elements which lead to the production of a phenomenon and postulated the criterion of choice as the only way of delimiting the field of investigation. Causal explanation is thus delimited and enclosed in a finite series of elements, as the totality of causal elements made up from an infinite multiplicity inevitably escapes investigation. We arrive at the basic problem of grounding the scientific autonomy of sociological investigation. Once a series of relations has been defined by means of a choice, how can one manage to establish that it is these and not others which have determined the given phenomenon? Weber's answer lies in recourse to a system we might call indirect testing, through the use of hypothetical processes or conceptual ideal types, obtained by excluding a specific element from the real process, and which permits a comparison between the real process and the potential process hypothetically constructed.

From this comparison it should be possible to establish the causal importance of a particular moment in the context of the process under investigation, and to isolate in the multiplicity of the empirically given some elements that could be included in a noncontradictory framework. By this means Weber arrived at the construction of his most important heuristic instrument, the ideal type. This was a difficult construction, prepared and made possible through a particular conception of sociology as "understanding sociology" (verstehende Soziologie), and by resolving the antithesis between "general" and "individual" by means of the notion of the "typical."

For Weber, sociology and the conceptual system that guarantees its scientific character manifest themselves characteristically as suspended between nature and history; that is, between a systematic discourse logically closed, standardized and (ahistorically) nomothetic, and the opening toward the unforeseeable and unique, produced by the process of history — not wholly standardizable and basically ideographic. Sociology is the science of culture, and the reality of Kultur is none other than history, Geschichte, or, more precisely, the history present in it, "history" in the broader sense as "historical life." In contrast to social science, natural science only aims at isolating "general" laws, and is not concerned with "understanding" the individual. Social science on the other hand wants "to understand by explaining" the individual.

Weber brings out the fact that our "lived," "intuitive," "evident" life (Erlebnis), abstractions and connections of a conceptual-general type, are always present in an intuitive manner.[21] The task of the social scientist lies in explicating the whole of the "intuitiveness" implicit in "experienced" life, to bring it to full "awareness" (Bewusstsein) of itself. In other words, Weber does not see why social science should not be able to develop clearly the "general" part intrinsic in concrete existence itself. Therefore there is no reason for a sharp contrast between "intuitive" and "conceptual," even though a distinction must be kept between them, one that indeed marks out the distinction between life and science — the latter being simply the conscious development of the "general" component of life itself.

It must be remembered that for Weber the "intuitive datum" is the "content" of the concept which it delineates, only one level lower than that of the "critical knowledge" of the concept itself. One sees that this is why the basic problem is what he points to as the logical problem of the relation between the concept and its content.[22] In the field of cultural sciences, the difference of their logical structure as against that of the natural sciences derives from the basis of values. In the natural sciences "valid laws" are sought and established. On the other hand, in the social sciences, in their "logical" aspect there exists the "conceptual possibility," while in their "effective" aspect there is an "objective possibility" of "testable connections capable of interpretation."

While in the natural sciences there is, so to speak, a lawfully valid picture of reality, in the social sciences there is simply an "interpretation" of it. This interpretation involves the "relation to values," the "awareness" of values, which are always manifested in an individual manner. The ultimate aim of the social sciences is thus the knowledge ("consciousness") of these values and the "individual," seen as contents, or as expounded in specific terms of structures and historically determined attitudes.

In this respect, it should be pointed out that for sociological analysis, "evidence," or "interpreting the evidential," can only have the weight of an hypothesis or "ideal-typical conceptual formation." This is the most interesting feature of Weber's creation. In fact, we may see from this, as will be clarified later, that the "typical-ideal concept" does not have the same value as a "natural law," assumed to be universally and necessarily valid and thus incontestable, but is rather one of many "possible evidential interpretations" of reality, with which the concept cannot simplistically, naturalistically be identified.

On the other hand, in this regard Weber's analogy between cultural and natural sciences concerning the categorial-cognitive dualism of "evidence" and "empirical validity" must be emphasized. The social or cultural sciences can also have "empirical validity," though with all the qualitative differences mentioned above, bearing constantly in mind also that this "empirical validity" is not the same as — and indeed, as a "psychological," individual element, conflicts with — the "evidence." To achieve "empirical validity," referral of the phenomenon under investigation to the conceptual system of the researcher — that is, to his value assumptions — is essential.

Sociology
in Relation to Nature,
Biography and History

From the standpoint of the evolution of sociological thought, Weber's historical merit lies basically in his having restored to the individual the responsibility for choice on the basis of his personal interests. After Comte's socio-centrism and the "factualism" of Durkheim, and in opposition to the pretentious universalism of the sociology of the "determinant factor," Weber rediscovered the importance of individual decisions and the initially basic function of personal interest. At the same time he tried to repair the fracture between the sciences of nature and those of culture, made by the romantic tradition. He was the first to grasp that "social facts are not things," that they are unitary realities, both very real and ambiguous. They are mixed realities in flux, more actions in progress than congealed and completed facts, in which contradictory, standardized and unique, quantitative and qualitative aspects are manifested as mixed together and confused. Seen in this light, they make up the object of the sociology of understanding.

The first definition of the "understanding sociology" (verstehende Soziologie) appeared in the 1913 essay "Some categories of 'understanding' sociology." He referred to it also in "The meaning of 'ethical neutrality' in the sociological and economic sciences" (1917), but it is above all elaborated in the posthumous Wirtschaft und Gesellschaft, a work published in 1921 but reflected upon and studied in the years 1911–13.

What is the task of sociology as a science? At the beginning of Wirtschaft und Gesellschaft Weber states: "Sociology (in the sense in which this highly ambiguous word is used here) is a science concerning itself with the interpretive understanding of social action and thereby with a causal explanation of its course and consequences."[1] Further on he says that "the specific task of sociological analysis or of that of the other sciences of action, ... is the inter-

pretation of action in terms of its subjective meaning."[2] The most
interesting element, the real "understanding" of sociology, concerns this "action in terms of its subjective meaning." One arrives
at an "understanding" of what Weber describes as "subjectively
intended" or "subjectively referred" meaning by means of "generalizations from experience." What is involved here is the "understanding" of connections of meaning — that is, the comprehension
(Verstehen) of an intelligible "sequence of motivation," clarification (Erklären) of which can serve as "an explanation of the actual
course of behavior." Thus, "explanation" — in a discipline concerned
with the meaning of behavior — requires that the researcher understand the Sinnzusammenhang, the "connection of meaning," the "complex of meaning in which an actual course of understandable action
thus interpreted belongs."[3]

The object of "understanding" sociology is thus an "action" endowed with a "subjectively referred meaning." This action is none
other than the action of "individual persons." (Further on in fact
we read: "But for the subjective interpretation of action in sociological work these collectivities must be treated as solely the
resultants and modes of organization of the particular acts of individual persons, since these alone can be treated as agents in a
course of subjectively understandable action.") Only individuals
can give "subjective meaning" to social action, which thus, being
the action of individuals, is itself individual and always manifest
in a singular manner. However, while this social behavior does
indeed have a meaning subjectively related to certain individuals,
it is naturally social in that it is "directed toward the past, present or intended future of other individuals."[4] The "interpretive
understanding" of sociology is directed toward the "meaning," or "the
average of, or an approximation to, the actually intended meaning."[5]

Social science is distinguished from natural science in that its
subject matter is not nature but society, not the objective but the
subjective, not the mechanically standardizable but the nonrepeat-
able, not an immobile, fixed structure but the behavioral variable,
action; not the unrelated but the related and the relationship. However, social science and natural science do have one thing in common: both impose order on their objects through general concepts.
Insofar as they propose themselves valid for everything, as conventions of abstract thought, these general concepts permit universal agreement. However, to clarify, one stresses that this is
above all a clarity and awareness of the nature, limits, and logical
and cognitive scope of these concepts; and thus the possibility of

disagreement and polemics, though always on a plane both critical and clear for all. By virtue of these cognitive means sociology is presented as a science, as valid as any natural science.

There is thus a difference in subject matter; however, this does not mean total heterogeneity on the logical level. The means are the same (concepts), but the aims are different. While for natural science, concepts and general laws are ends in themselves or are identified with the end of research itself, in sociology (as for all the sciences of "culture") they are instruments for attaining the subject matter — that is, social action in its specific configuration.

Sociology helps us to acquire a clear awareness of social reality with all its historical implications, and thus also of the past as well as the present and future, though always in relation to contemporary, actual implications. Of course, full understanding of the latter also involves that of the past, history as historiography. However, if history cannot provide us with a scientific, detached view of the present, either for want of specific investigatory techniques or of a critical "distance" from it, sociology may be successful in this. For this reason too, one cannot say that Weber takes sociology to be a science auxiliary to historiography.

Weber's constant referral to "in der Gegenwart" (in the present), his continual reference to contemporary social issues in his sociological studies (these indeed always aspire to be a function of today and today's society; see, for example, this expression in the essays in Religionssoziologie), confirm my interpretation. They also demonstrate that when Weber speaks of history and historiography, he is really talking about history in the "broader sense of the term," in the sense of "historical life." This expression broadens the scope of "history" to make it coextensive with the "reality" to be studied, which in turn is Kultur, to be explained according to the understanding of its internal connections and genesis.

Historiography, on the other hand, is a distinct, autonomous science, which, like sociology, may be included in the area of the other sciences of "civilization" and also shows some connections with them. However, Weber is principally concerned with establishing the relations and differences between historiography and sociology. Both aim at "interpretive understanding" — the former, of the meaning and connection of the meaning really intended in the particular case, and the latter (as already noted), of the meaning or connection of meaning on the average, approximately.[6] "We have taken for granted that sociology seeks to formulate type con-

cepts and generalized uniformities of empirical processes. This
distinguishes it from history, which is oriented to the causal analysis and explanation of individual actions, structures, and person-
alities possessing cultural significance."[7]

One should not be taken in by the mistaken interpretation of this
passage whereby there is almost a theorization of a contrast between sociology and historiography in terms of the contrast between the "general" and the "individual," according to a contemporary interpretation of the relation between history and sociology.
We have in fact already seen that sociology too is a "science of
individual reality," and thus aims at the explanation and "understanding" of reality. As we have mentioned, one can only say that
if it is true that "concepts" or the "general rules of development"
are rightly those of both types of science, they are elaborated
directly and according to specific techniques only by sociology,
which aims at understanding individual, singular reality, inasmuch
as "The empirical material which underlies the concepts of sociology consists to a very large extent, though by no means exclusively, of the same concrete processes of action which are dealt
with by historians."[8] Thus sociology provides the "laws," the
awareness and "unequivocalness" of concepts, to the "historico-
causal knowledge of phenomena of cultural importance."

Why, then, is sociology able to elaborate these "laws" or "concepts"? Whence this unusual privilege? Basically it is because
in sociology's systematic approach one finds a distinction between
the two meanings of "general," or "allgemein," namely (a) in the
sense of "general" concept, hence with a logical value, better expressed in the German "generell," and (b) in the sense of "universally valid," that is, of the unconditional "universal" validity of
values, well expressed in the German "universell," and thus of
"normative" value. Sociology indeed is concerned with discovering
"within the realm of social action certain empirical uniformities..., that is, courses of action that are repeated by the actor
or (simultaneously) occur among numerous actors since the subjective meaning is meant to be the same."[9] The true subject matter of sociology is indeed marked by this "homogeneity," the "universal" referral or relation to "norms" and "values."

Clearly, history and sociology have two points in common (the
concept, and the subjective, or individual or "intended meaning,"
to be understood differently, however, in the two disciplines),
which end up interfering in the logical process of "understanding"
(or interpreting) by explaining the actually intended meaning for

concrete historical action.[10] "Both for sociology in the present sense, and for history, the object of cognition is the subjective meaning-complex of action."[11] As for historiography, this is concerned with "the average of, or an approximation to, the actually intended meaning."[12]

The elaboration of general concepts is, however, a logico-instrumental question that concerns both disciplines. Sociology gives us the "homogeneous," the "typical," while historiography provides the "individual." From an abstraction, the concept is derived as a logical tool to penetrate and grasp the realities studied by historiography as well as by sociology.

Sociology, like historiography, works out and uses a system of concepts. Both sciences also have a common subject matter — social action and human initiative — in their specific historical determination. However, these basic common characteristics cannot justify any summary reduction of one to the other. The reductionist claim, as I have had occasion to remark elsewhere,[13] is the result of a misunderstanding. This involves on the one hand a conception of sociological analysis that is still Comtean in nature, systematic in the omnicomprehensive sense, which puts itself forward logically as the "science of sciences"; and on the other, historical research that actually coincides with the whole of man and all his possible creations, or all reality. The latter is seen as raised up in the various phases of its development into the supreme manifestation of absolute spirit. Sociology as a closed system has for some time now yielded in the face of the demand for specific social investigations centered on circumscribed and scientifically relevant phenomena. Something analogous has happened in the case of historicism, with new critical demands to do justice to the complexity and basic indeterminateness of the human world, to make absolute the moments of time in which the absolute spirit might materialize; a founding characteristic of romantic-idealist historicism has been eaten away at the roots. That is, it presents itself as both the conclusion and the closure of the course of history, and at the same time argues, at once contradictorily, for the need of transcending what it affirms, on the basis of that very proposition which should be negated.[14]

Once this reduction of sociological analysis has been digested into the context of historical development, sociology takes on a purely instrumental value while at the same time it loses any really cognitive value. It is demoted to a convenient system of classification. As Antoni usefully reminds us, "as earlier for

Vico, for Croce too the only form of knowledge was historical knowledge."[15]   The other sciences did not provide knowledge; at the most they could provide classes and laws useful for summarizing experience for practical purposes, and for cataloging phenomena.

The bias towards totality is basic and helps to explain the tendency to reductionism. This bias has found a particularly skillful critic in Karl R. Popper.[16] He notes that there is a basic ambiguity in the use of the word "whole." In fact, the term is normally used in two senses. The first indicates the totality of all the properties or aspects of something, and especially all the reciprocal relations between its constitutive parts. The second points to some special properties or aspects of the thing in question — that is, those that make it appear as an organized structure rather than a mere conglomeration. In this second sense, the term has been used as an expression of a key concept by psychologists of the form, or Gestalt. For them, the objects possessing such an organized structure are something more than the sum of their parts. The ambiguity of total or global conceptions, which by definition tend to ingest all of reality in certain schemas without leaving anything behind, rests basically on the confusion between the two senses.[17] In these conceptions, the two meanings of the term "whole" are used interchangeably. In other words, while one recognizes that every scientific analysis is necessarily selective, and thus is unable to consider all aspects and properties of a given thing or phenomenon, one nonetheless tends on the other hand to present the analysis of the "whole," viewed as a group of meaningful aspects and not all aspects of the thing, as though in fact it were the positive, conclusive inclusion of all the known characteristics making up a given historico-social phenomenon. It is thanks to this logical leap that it is possible to speak of absolute historicism and that to consider totality as an object of scientific analysis, both from a sociological and a historiographic point of view, is expressed as a new theology.

The collaboration between sociology and history may, in this regard, be presented not only as a natural consequence of the principle of division of labor between neighboring disciplines, but also as a useful antidote to the conception of history as a flux of happenings, endowed with automatic organizational powers, something necessary and necessitating. For such a conception, precedent and consequent are justified in so absolute a way as to leave no margin for unforeseeable individual initiatives and to allow of no recognition of biographical data. On the other hand, there is no doubt that personal documents and autobiographies may, for the historian and sociologist, constitute empirical material that is fundamental for purposes of description and interpretation.

As for sociology, much time has elapsed since the era when Thomas and Znaniecki argued:

> We are safe in saying that personal life-records, as complete as possible, constitute the perfect type of sociological material, and that if social science has to use other materials at all it is only because of the practical difficulty of obtaining at the moment a sufficient number of such records to cover the totality of sociological problems, and of the enormous amount of work demanded for an adequate analysis of all the personal materials necessary to characterize the life of a social group. [18]

I have noted elsewhere that Thomas's and Znaniecki's monumental work — though its limitations are obvious in light of the criticisms of Herbert Blumer and other scholars — may still constitute a valid example of the use of personal documents on a huge scale. Thomas in the United States and Znaniecki in Poland were able to collect, put in systematic order, and then publish seven hundred and sixty-four letters, focusing their attention on the changes and adjustments imposed on primary groups of Polish peasants by the process of industrialization, their gradual proletarianization, and finally the emigration of relatives. Critical analysis of the letters, autobiographies, and other personal documents produced results of great interest from a substantive point of view, which have not, however, escaped the expression of severe reservations from the methodological point of view. Among others, Herbert Blumer observed that the autobiographical material and the letters and documents of various kinds that Thomas and Znaniecki collected certainly helped to back up — and to some extent better to define — their theoretical propositions and hypotheses. However, one cannot argue that empirical material of this kind can prove these propositions and hypotheses in any way. In other words, Blumer argues that the autobiographical material collected only complemented the knowledge the authors already possessed about the world of the Polish peasant and about the effects of emigration and industrialization on preindustrial human groups. [19]

In my view, the use of autobiographical material and personal documents as spontaneous, first-person descriptions of the experiences, beliefs, and actions of an individual, is of great importance in casting light on the background of a problem or particular social phenomenon, situating it in its correct perspective; and, further, in focusing the theme of research and laying out the basic, quantitatively measurable data that will be included in the formulation of the hypothesis to be tested. In this sense, autobiographical material and personal documents are precious, even indispensable, for "background research," in that they provide indications of behavior and attitudes that may be expressed in rigorous terminology, which lends itself to classification and quantitative testing.[20]

Autobiographical material thus constitutes a body of primary data which, in the economy of research, has a basic function. It is in fact true that a highly elaborated statistical analysis can in some cases lead to the mathematical determination of interesting correlation indices between very dissimilar empirical variables: only mathematical instruments can unearth these, giving rise to new, significant hypotheses. However, it is rather rare to create hypotheses on the basis of correlation indices. These indices in fact, for the most part, help to test hypotheses already formulated according to the general model of probability theory. The autobiographical element brings sociology back to a discourse that in certain significant ways is naturalistic. In fact, autobiographies make important tendencies "break through" the raw magma of undifferentiated behavior. As Harold D. Lasswell rightly observes, "The life history is a natural history, and a natural history is concerned with facts which are developmentally significant."[21]

The question sociological analysis then faces is that of determining a nonarbitrary periodization of a life history viewed in such a way as to see its principal periods of development and identify its characteristic matrices of behavior. What makes the greater part of autobiographies and life histories collected by sociologists meaningless, if not scientifically misleading, is precisely this lack of heuristic concern. Autobiography thus becomes presented and evaluated as a suggestive tranche de vie, interesting for its curious or exceptional characteristics rather than its heuristic value, and rarely free from a second-rate literary tone. Such a result is largely inevitable when life histories are not collected with attention to the economic, social, and cultural context in which they are placed. However, this awareness is impossible if the researcher does not hold a theory of personality that can provide the essential points of reference to describe and understand the complex, interwoven body of relations that bind the biography of an individual — seen as the meaningful record of his development — to the basic characteristics of his personality and

also to the family and other primary social groups to which he belongs as well as to the broader framework of the institutional
structure of the society in which he lives. Without this integrated
approach it appears difficult to avoid one or another of the classic
fallacies that have marked the development of sociology. On the
one hand, we have a macrosociological, structural analysis, by
definition unable to grasp the meaningful psychological element,
and thus continually exposed to the danger of pseudo-systematic
formalism. On the other, we have sociological research concerned
with collecting and evaluating individual behavior, but basically
unable to provide us with anything more than a gallery of carica-
tures, if not indeed the dilution of every real sociological problem
into a series of psychologistic formulas, basically unverifiable and
arbitrary.

The Ideal Type

Weber used a specific conceptual instrument to permit sociology to grasp the unique, characterizing element of social action in the framework of the structures that condition it institutionally and historically: this is the "ideal type." The theory of the "ideal type" is the supreme moment in Weber's methodological thought, the instrument used in his famous studies; yet, at the same time, it brings out unresolved difficulties, ambiguities, omissions, and contradictions.

Talcott Parsons, among others, has capitalized on the traditional criticisms leveled against Weber. What are "ideal types"? Is it enough to define them as points of reference or as deliberately emphasized aspects of human behavior? Are we dealing with an experimental category drawn out by empirical research, or a concept properly so-called, and thus provided with its own internal, rigorous logic? If it is only an instrument, how can it be elaborated? If "type" has the aspect of uniformity and repeatability, what does "ideal" mean in this context? Can it be understood as "rational" or "abstract," or does it mean "desirable"?[1] As it is impossible to find exhaustive responses to such questions in Weber, Parsons finds confirmation for his own conviction as to Weber's insufficiently systematic nature — seeming not to realize that he is reproving Weber precisely for his real merit.

For Weber, in fact, the conceptual apparatus of sociology must be capable of grasping the "typical" or "homogeneous" element in historical phenomena in order to deal with them scientifically — that is, to provide an "explanation" or "causal imputation." However, a logic or methodology of concepts cannot serve this purpose, as this simply repeats the traditional principle (Aristotelian in origin) genus proximum — differentia specifica, characteristic of "axiomatic disciplines which use syllogisms."[2]

It is therefore necessary to establish a new method capable of guaranteeing the designation "sciences" to the disciplines of culture, especially sociology. Weber confronts this requirement by constructing "ideal types." Ideal types are "conventional types" (that is, established abstractly and conventionally), "clear and understandable by reference to an ideal type."[3] They are intelligible because one sees in them a conscious contact between "understanding" (verstehen) and "experiencing" (erfahren), here synonymous with "explanation" (erklären), between "value" and "concept," between "having to be" (or "having to behave") and empirical "being."

First, however, it is necessary to specify the sense in which the ideal-typical concept, by way of which one obtains a synthesis of "objective" and "subjective," "general" and "individual," passing through the plane of the "typical," is really "ideal." In fact, there are in Weber two meanings of "ideal" — a normative and a logical one. The qualification of "typical concept" by "ideal" has only a logical value, in that it is presented as abstract from the reality of which "values" and "norms" — that is, "having to be" — are part.

"Ideal types," however, aim at showing only "what is" on the empirical level, not "what should be." If "values" enter into their consideration, they enter only by way of the checking and "distance" of what Weber describes as the "technical critique of values." In other words, this is the "knowledge" or "awareness" at which empirico-objective science aims and whose "ideal-typical" concepts are the instruments and means of investigation. As Weber says: "the scientific treatment of value-judgments,.... of these ultimate standards, which are manifested in concrete value-judgments to the level of explicitness is the utmost that the scientific treatment of value-judgments can do without entering into the realm of speculation."[4]

As an example of the "ideal" contrasted with the "real" one could take "commander," and set up a "type" who could act "without error" in a given situation if he had a "representation" and "knowledge" of it that was ideally, logically, and rationally coherent. A comparison between the given "general situation" and the "ideal-typical construction" (the "type" of the commander) could give us the differences between them, as well as the extent of the "approaching" (Annäherung) or approximation of the "real" action of the commander to that of the "ideal-typical construction."

To clarify the nature of the relation between "value" (or "norm" as evaluative "ideal") and "ideal-type concept," it would be useful to read the passage in the <u>Wissenschaftslehre</u> where Weber asserts that "the term 'value' — that unfortunate child of misery of our science — can be given an unambiguous meaning only as an ideal type."[5] When one is faced with a given reality, it is obvious that in order to see it in a "distanced" manner one can take up various points of observation, from which other different perspectives, all partial and nonexhaustive, are revealed. On the other hand, in order to formulate a hypothesis about the nature and real causal value of a given phenomenon, one must proceed by way of various "ideal-typical" perspectives, that is, "unilateral" ones insofar as they are abstracted from the complete reality of the phenomenon in question. Indeed, the ideal type is not a hypothesis but rather tends to formulate or suggest hypotheses.

Obviously, from a "unilateral" point of view one "stresses" certain "features" or "elements" and passes over others as secondary. In other words, some features are isolated from a context or complex of elements. As a result of this process of "isolation" and "abstraction," some connection is established between the "isolated" or "stressed" features and certain of their relationships — whence, from a "unilateral" point of view, there is produced what Weber describes as an "ideal frame," "model," or abstract "schema," i.e., one that is a "utopia," "unreal" in that it is partial and also a "heuristic means" to understand a reality that itself is much more complex and polyvalent than the "fantastic picture."

This "ideal frame" or "model" gives us a "genetic definition of the content of the concept."[6] It is not reality, but aims at its understanding. Its goal is to illustrate and make pragmatically intelligible the specific character (<u>Eigenart</u>)[7] of a particular phenomenon. The sociologist can obtain this only by elaborating various unilateral "ideal-type concepts" constructed from different points of view, since the discursive nature of our chain of intellectual modifications postulates such a conceptual shorthand.[8] The ideal type

is a conceptual construct (<u>Gedankenbild</u>) which is neither historical reality nor even the "true" reality. It is even less fitted to serve as a schema under which a real situation or action is to be subsumed as one <u>instance</u>. It has the significance of a purely ideal <u>limiting</u> concept with which the real situation or action is compared and surveyed for the explication of certain of its significant components.[9]

With respect to the ideal type, we can establish the measure of the "deviation" (<u>Ablenkung</u> or <u>Abweichung</u>) of reality from the "type," or its approximation to it. The advantage of the "ideal-typical concept" lies in the clarity it offers, as it aims at providing representation with a univocal means of expression. It has the advantage of a clear, critical terminology insofar as it is univocal. But how is the "ideal type" constructed?

An ideal type is formed by the one-sided <u>accentuation</u> of one or more points of view and by the synthesis of a great many diffuse, discrete, more or less present and occasionally absent <u>concrete individual</u> phenomena, which are arranged according to those one-sidedly emphasized viewpoints into a unified <u>analytical</u> construct (<u>Gedankenbild</u>). [10]

It is clear, therefore, that the "ideal type" is a heuristic means for the purpose of investigating a certain type of phenomenon and is oriented in a particular "direction"; it is valid until the need arises to elaborate a better one, i.e., one that better corresponds to the needs of the researcher.

In fact, these "ideal-typical concepts" have the advantage of "univocality of the conceptual content," but they vary as "our scientific interest" varies and with the change in the "meaning" of our "relationships to values." They do not propose anything other than the critico-genetic investigation of values and their relation to the historical world and preconstituted "methodological knowledge," or the complex of "general empirical rules" or "rules of experience" already known, the known ideal types, valid and accepted.

Determining the ideal type for Weber is thus tied to emphasizing a given aspect of empirical reality at the expense of others, a process of "utopian rationalization" that avoids the generalization of common features. The ideal type is thus something other than empirical reality, though it appears in relation with it as the instrument of explanation of phenomena in their individuality.

Weber cites as an example the idea of "urban economy." Here is an ideal type reached not by making a selection of the economic principles that actually obtained in the cities observed, but rather through unilateral emphasis on certain points of view and through the joining together of specific phenomena corresponding to those points of view, enclosed in a conceptual framework unitary in itself. Because of its abstract character this conceptual framework appears as a utopia, since in all its purity it cannot be located in reality. According to Weber,

It is a conceptual construct (<u>Gedankenbild</u>) which is neither historical reality nor even the "true" reality. It is even less fitted to serve as a schema under which a real situation or action is to be subsumed as one <u>instance</u>. It has the significance of a purely ideal <u>limiting</u> concept with which the real situation or action is <u>compared</u> and surveyed for the explication of certain of its significant components. [11]

He argues that for a "representation" the use of such concepts is indispensable, even if our "fantasy" can dispense with them. Syntheses of historically operative ideas such as "liberalism," "methodism," or "socialiam" have an ideal-typical nature, which we elaborate on the basis of fundamental directing principles, and which have come to us only in an incomplete form, without clear conceptual connections. According to Weber:

All expositions, for example, of the "essence" of Christianity,are ideal types enjoying only a necessarily very relative and problematic validity when they are intended to be regarded as the historical portrayal of empirically existing facts. On the other hand, such presentations are of great value for research and of high systematic value for expository purposes when they are used as conceptual instruments for <u>comparison</u> with and the <u>measurement</u> of reality. [12]

The language spoken by the historian, he continues, by reason of its need for discursive clarity, expresses these conceptual frameworks in hundreds of words.

Weber takes the battle of Marathon as an example of the use of ideal types in historical research. This battle decided between two possibilities: on the one hand the development of a religious-theoretical culture under the aegis of a Persian protector, and on the other the victory of the Hellenic spiritual world, for which it represented the indispensable precondition. Without evaluating this possibility it would be impossible to understand the phenomenon, and "there would in truth be no reason why we should not rate that decisive contest equally with a scuffle between two tribes of Kaffirs or Indians." [13] Already, the first step toward historical judgment is one of abstraction, of analysis and conceptual isolation of empirical elements. "Even this first step thus transforms the given 'reality' into a 'mental construct' in order to make it into an historical fact. In Goethe's words, 'theory' is involved in the 'fact.'" [14]

For Weber, the historical significance of a fact is not established by the setting out of what the historian finds before him. The fact acquires validity only insofar as it adds to reality the patrimony of our knowledge, our nomological type of experience, on the basis, that is, of a conceptual framework, abstraction in the double sense of isolation and generalization.

The sociologist too, like the historian, uses these conceptual frameworks; but "theoretical concepts of sociology are ideal types not only from the objective point of view, but also in their application to subjective processes."[15] In fact, sociology tries to formulate and express in theoretical concepts even irrational, mystical, and affective phenomena. "In all cases, rational or irrational, sociological analysis both abstracts from reality and at the same time helps us to understand it, in that it shows with what degree of approximation a concrete historical phenomenon can be subsumed under one or more of these concepts."[16]

Real action generally develops in semi-consciousness of its "intentional meaning." The individual agent is mostly instinctive, or acts from habit, save in sporadic cases of homogeneous mass action. Effectively aware and clear action is for Weber the ultimate case. Nonetheless it is the task of sociology to elaborate its concepts by way of explanation and classification of the possible intentional meaning, as if action was in fact proceeding in a consciously oriented manner.

This does not mean that the theory of the ideal type presupposes the rationality of the world. Rather, by using the theory, the researcher approaches concrete reality as nearly as possible, revealing the irrational deviations and the causes that determine them as they interfere in the ideal rational operation. Weber explains: "We should emphasize that the idea of an ethical imperative, or a 'model' of what 'ought' to exist is to be carefully distinguished from the analytical construct, which is 'ideal' in the strictly logical sense of the term."[17] This, consequently, does not give rise to a new break between the ideal types of pure rationality and concrete historical material. For Weber, the construction of "conceptual frameworks" is not dangerous for the purposes of unprejudiced research, since it is not an end but a means of research. However, one must take care that the ideal type not be ascribed empirical validity (as is the tendency) invading the sphere of interpretation and thus becoming a value judgment. An ideal type has no connection with "perfection" save in the purely logical sense, and it is independent in relation to evaluative judgment. To the extent that the ideal type relates to historical "individualities," it

has the function of revealing typical features in general characteristics. Its application should further clarify any confusion, in the
field of reality, between the idea and the ideal of any historical
fact.

Weber gives as an example the ideal-typical construction of the
phenomenon "liberalism." We may regard the liberal phenomenon
either as a political regime or as a human attitude; that is, we may
construct an ideal type of the "idea" or of the "ideal" of liberalism,
and hence gain knowledge of the distinction in the sphere of ideal
conceptions between how they were thought of by men in the past
and our own current ideal types.

Once more, it is Weber's concern to distinguish clearly between
the spheres of being and of what should be. The concern rests on
the fact that Weber is wholly aware that the distinction is precari-
ous. Faced with the danger that conceptual frameworks may be
transformed into value judgments, Weber warns: "the elementary
duty of scientific self-control and the only way to avoid serious and
foolish blunders requires a sharp, precise distinction between the
logically comparative analysis of reality by ideal types in the logical sense and the value judgment of reality on the basis of
ideals."[18] Ideal-typical formulations should not contain, consciously or otherwise, ideals to which the researcher refers the
facts studied, for purposes of valuation. But is this possible?
When he argues that the way these syntheses are made — the way
contemporaries in various historical periods construct their ideas
— is of eminently practical importance, Weber seems to stress
the utopian nature of his distinction. In several places he observes
how the practical idea in which one believes, insofar as it is valid
or should be valid, and the theoretical ideal type constructed for
cognitive purposes, draw near and tend to be transformed into each
other.

For example, ideal types can be concerned with lines of development, but precisely from that there arises the danger of confusing
ideal type and reality. For this reason, he stresses, in order not
to confuse theory and history, or even conflate them, one must
rigorously maintain the distinction between ideal-typical construction (which permits us systematically and validly to refer a historical process to its causes) and history itself.

The ideal-typical concept is thus a "unitary framework," "imaginary," logically constructed on the basis of the principle of "non-
contradiction." "This conceptual framework joins determinate
relations and determinate processes of historical life in a cosmos

of conceptual connections, without contradiction."[19] This too shows the "unreality" of ideal-typical concepts, which present only some abstract "analogies" and are based on a logic of "as if" (als ob).[20] Nonetheless, it might be possible that an "ideal type" could be concretely verified; but that is highly improbable and must be established each time.

If, as we have said, ideal types have as their purpose knowledge of individual reality not only in its specific elements but also in the connections between these, that is, their causal and historical relations, then we must clarify how the process of "causal imputation" (in which the system of ideal types originates and toward which it tends to move) develops. When we speak of these "connections" we move from consideration of simple ideal-type elements to ideal-typical links between them, which means that from simple "ideal types" we move to "relations between ideal types."

What is presented to the sociologist as an object of knowledge is, as we have seen, the "world of culture as historically given." This involves knowing concrete "historical individuals," the concrete forms of given historical reality. As Weber says, for knowledge of reality we must refer to the constellation in which the elements of reality are to be found, "ideal-typically" presented and gathered into a cultural phenomenon that is historically meaningful for us. If we wish to explain this individual grouping causally, we must always refer to other groupings, equally individual, as a basis for explanation — naturally, through the use of ideal-typical concepts. Once certain "laws" have been established by ideal-typical methods (that is, those that make up "nomological knowledge"), and certain factors have been discovered by ideal-typical means, the establishment of those laws and factors is in every single case the first of the many operations that lead us to knowledge. "The analysis of the historically given individual configuration of those 'factors' and their significant concrete interaction, conditioned by their historical context and especially the rendering intelligible of the basis and type of this significance," is the second task of scientific knowledge, which "must be achieved, it is true, by the utilization of the preliminary analysis but...is nonetheless an entirely new and distinct task."[21]

In other words, a certain "nomological knowledge" is given in the science of culture, but it must not be taken as an absolute. Further, insofar as it helps us to know analytically "a historically given individual group," it is multifunctional, provisional, and abstract. The third task lies in the return to the specific individual

characteristics of such groupings as are meaningful for the present, going back into the past as far as possible, and in "their historical explanation by antecedent and equally individual configura-
tions." The fourth task consists in "the prediction of possible future constellations."[22]

To clarify the method of development of the process of "causal
imputation," one must first grasp the meaning of the categories
"adequate causation" and "objective possibility." The scientist
asks himself: "How in general is the attribution of a concrete effect to an individual 'cause' possible and realizable in principle
in view of the fact that in truth an infinity of causal factors have
conditioned the occurrence of the individual 'event.' "[23] Further
on he says: "The possibility of selection from among the infinity
of the determinants is conditioned, first, by the mode of our historical interest." This involves, then, "causally imputing" only
those "elements" or "aspects" that from specific points of view
offer a "universal meaning"; that is, "essential elements." Thus,
causal imputation involves a "series of abstractions." In fact,
finding these "essential elements" really means selecting some
that are interesting from our points of view and passing over
others. Essential elements thus become "causally relevant" for
us. The "ideal-typical concept" really is involved in a "series of
abstractions" of this kind. The sociologist merely continually
formulates "judgments concerning possibilities."[24] In order to
establish the "causally relevant" event, in the sense that this be
the "real cause" of a given fact from among infinite conditions, the
sociologist creates "imaginative constructs" by the disregard-
ing of one or more of those elements of "reality" that are actually present, and by the mental construction of a course of
events that is altered through modification in one or more "conditions."[25]

These "conceptual frameworks" and this "conceptual construction" are the same as "ideal-typical concepts." In fact, the "first
step" toward "causal imputation" is already a process of "abstraction" and "conceptual isolation," which breaks down the "empirical
given" into "elements" viewed as "a complex of possible causal
relationships." The most interesting observation is this:

we so decompose the "given" into "components" that every one of them is
fitted into an "empirical rule"; hence, that it can be determined what effect
each of them, with others present as "conditions," "could be expected" to have,
in accordance with an empirical rule.[26]

The category of "objective possibility," the logical basis for every judgment of possibility, is an abstraction — or, in other words, a reasoning ab absurdo, which tries to establish "what would have happened" in the case of excluding or changing certain conditions. Here, the "as if" of the ideal type returns, as has been discussed above.

A judgment of "possibility" in the sense in which the expression is used here, means, then, the continuous reference to "empirical rules" (Erfahrungsregeln). The category of "possibility" is thus not used in its negative form. It is, in other words, not an expression of our ignorance or incomplete knowledge in contrast with the assertive or apodictic judgment. Rather, to the contrary, it signifies here the reference to a positive knowledge of the "laws of events," to our "nomological" knowledge, as they say. [27]

The given facts belonging to the "historical situation" are, on the other hand, our "ontological" knowledge.

We are dealing with a verification or a test that follows the normal procedures of scientific research. One attempts to isolate an element within the context of an historical connection, then to eliminate or modify it, and finally to estimate, on the basis of a "general rule of experience," whether the process thus changed would have been able to develop in the same way. If it could have done so, then it is clear that the element excluded had no causal "relevance," and if not, the reverse is true. [28] Thus one goes on to exclude or in various ways to modify first this and then that element, until one manages to find the "causally relevant" element and establish the process of "adequate causation" of an effect to a cause which can provide us with a clear, objective, and valid picture of a historical connection. Here it is worthwhile stressing that the process of "causal imputation" has a teleological value, insofar as the "cause" is presented as a "means" and the "effect" as "end." [29] This is due to the fact that in the social sciences one is dealing with human action and a "subjectively referred action," which cannot therefore be explained simply by a naturalistic type of causal concept. Rather, this must be seen in terms of "meaning," i.e., the teleology of the actors.

Finally, one must consider the question of "conditions" and historical "conditionality" in the broad sense. In some scholars' view, Weber replaced the naturalistic notion of "cause" with that of "conditionality," and in such a way that he would never be able to know the concrete "cause" of a concrete fact but only its infinite "conditions," which "reciprocally condition" each other. In the

light of this interpretation, one must bear in mind that his discussion of "conditions" and their "infinity" is not a fact established
"from eternity," in the sense that to this individual shape all the
varied, infinite historical conditions have contributed. Rather, it
is only the reproduction, in causal explanation, of the idea of reality
as "intensively and extensively infinite multiplicity." This only
has a heuristic value — one, that is, of an "ultimate concept of the
ideal-typical kind," to which no effective truth and reality corresponds, precisely because it is constructed only logically and
"imaginatively." The same holds good for the "infinity" of conditions. If this were not so, we should have an absurd regressus in
indefinitum. One would never reach the end in an infinite process
of "causal imputation," and never, in any individual case, be able
to discover a particular, concrete, real cause. However, for
Weber, there is always such a "cause." His discussion of "infinity" is useful only as a heuristic means for not prejudicing from
the beginning, through any preconceived idea of cause or causal
"element," the "objective" course of causal imputation.

We may say that there are historical "conditions" and historical
"causes." Using the two categories of "causal imputation" we discover the "cause" or the "causes" (the relevant element or elements) of an individual, concrete historical process, isolated by a
specific, individual point of view. As a result one deduces an
ideal-typical, sociological law, which is hence partial and nonab-
solute. We might thus also say that history lives within sociology
and that as far as its historical-individual element is concerned,
sociology uses a concrete "causal" process, which then becomes
"conditional" to it. However, this "condition" exists relative to a
potential general, abstract theory of society, a systematic, phe-
nomenological science of society itself, beyond individual concrete
sociological investigations whose potentialities and validity are
not, as we have seen, to be sought in an omnicomprehensive, closed
system which runs the risk of falling into arbitrary formalism.

In The Protestant Ethic and the Spirit of Capitalism, for example, Weber tries to indicate the causal relation between religious and economic elements in a well-defined "historical individual phenomenon," capitalism. The relation between the
Protestant ethic and the "spirit of capitalism" is a question for
sociological investigation, to be worked out at the level of positive
research. Weber analyzes only one aspect of that relation, the influence of ethics on economics, but not the reverse. He admits that
economic conditions can also become determining causes, as

treated in the other studies in Religionssoziologie. Here too, however, the causal connections only serve comparatively better to
characterize Western development. Indeed, it is through this
"comparison" that we find that the Protestant ethic is an important
factor. Weber wants to find a "general law of experience," "the
influence of certain religious ideas on the development of an economic spirit, or the ethos of an economic system. In this case
we are dealing with the connection of the spirit of modern economic
life with the rational ethics of ascetic Protestantism."[30]

One might direct concrete investigation toward the establishment
of a "general law of experience" contrary to that set up by Weber,
but in such "laws" one will always be dealing with "conditions" and
never with "causes." For causes are to be found not in "general
laws" (which might be able to "generalize" causes, but without
recognizing other important facts in reality and so, hypostasizing
a single cause), but in the concrete, exemplary, specific investigations into determinate "historically individual phenomena." Here
it is acceptable to find a cause after the conscious establishment
of an "historically individual phenomenon," one that is isolated
precisely because one knows, is aware, that this cause is not
universal but individual and concrete. In our case, there is no
"general law," excluding the others, concerning the superiority
of the religious factor or religion itself over economics. There is
only the discovery of an "ideal-type" correlation between the two
factors, which remain quite distinct from one another and unmis-
takable. Weber calls this "to some extent equivocal," as indeed
one is not referring to a "general law" but to those religious elements of Western economic ethics that are peculiar to it, as distinct from others that are not.

Here Weber provides an important example of the interdisci-
plinary collaboration between historiography and sociology, in
which the two kinds of explanation, historical and sociological,
the causal and the conditional, come together to provide precious
reciprocal aid. First, we proceed to establish "a general rule of
experience" of a sociological kind, which may show us a conceptual
link between a religious fact and an economic one. This can be
shown only at the level of a concrete example, a causal-historical
imputation of a particular individual fact like that of the "Protestant ethic," and another individual fact such as modern "capitalism," or, more precisely, its "spirit."

In order to establish the stability of this "causal imputation,"
Weber was to go on (in the essays in Religionssoziologie) to a

comparison of the same kind of correlation, this same general rule of experience, in its two relations of conditioning, each reciprocal with the other, insofar as it is "historically" established outside Europe — in China, India and so on — as regards not only the economy but all the other structures that together make up society.

The relation of conditioning, or a different type of relation between phenomena, is consequently the conclusion he draws in defining the explanatory schema of the social sciences. The concepts of "connection" and "condition" make it clear that in the sphere of the social sciences, especially sociology, facts cannot be facts as such, in their static condition, but are rather facts as actions. The object of Weber's sociology is social actions, not collective but individual ones. Even in social formations of a collective kind — e.g., the state, companies, etc. — "Action in the sense of subjectively understandable orientation of behavior exists only as the behavior of one or more individual human beings."[31]

These collective formations are the representation of something present in the minds of real men, on the basis of which they direct their actions. Collective formations are thus reduced to the specific actions of individuals, and concepts such as "state," "association," "feudalism," and so forth designate categories of specific forms of human action in society. "We can accomplish something which is never attainable in the natural sciences, namely the subjective understanding of the action of the component individuals."[32] All this, Weber adds, is not in fact the case for other forms of explanation. He criticizes the "organic" method of sociology which explains social action by moving from the totality in order to interpret individual attitudes within it, just as one looks in physiology at the position of an organ in terms of the functioning of the whole organism. The battle against the organicist approach, as is rightly observed, "was the first defence of the essence of causal explanation to be attributed to historical knowledge, so as to be able to discover within it an internal guarantee of validity and appear as an empirical test of relations of cause and effect."[33]

Weber's sociology thus defines itself as "understanding" as it looks at the social fact in all its complexity; moreover, the task it sets itself is the understanding of the behavior of individuals, not simply as predetermined by their official function in the framework of the social system, but rather as regards the meaning they confer on and recognize in their activity. "Meaning" for Weber means grasping the meaningful connection into which one inserts an immediately intelligible action. He also decisively modifies the notion of "meaning," freeing it from the field of immediate, lived experience, and confirming its superiority over intuition. "Understanding" is no longer regarded as a simple "sympathetic insight," but an interpretation that must be tested at the empirical level. "Meaning" does not entail literal explanation, but taking relevant facts into consideration, though these may differ from those considered by history. Once more, inevitably, Weber returns to the concept of value. At the root of understanding there is an analysis of value which makes us understand the historical conditions and causal frameworks from which the phenomenon originates. Thus, "Every interpretation attempts to attain clarity and certainty, but no matter how clear an interpretation as such appears to be from the point of view of meaning, it cannot on this account claim to be the causally valid interpretation."[34]

In fact, human action is complex. There can be connections of meaning that conceal even from the active agent himself the real interconnections of his action. External processes of action that seem the same or similar to us may in reality arise from connections of meaning that are very different, inasmuch as men are driven by antithetical drives, conflicting motives, which we grasp in their entirety only in their final, effective result, post factum. For sociological interpretation, functional consideration of the parts of a totality is only a point of departure" for purposes of practical illustration and for provisional orientation. In these respects it is not only useful but indispensable. But at the same time if its cognitive value is overestimated and its concepts illegitimately 'reified,' it can be highly dangerous."[35]

Here Weber clearly takes his distance from Rickert's distinction between natural sciences and those of culture, which rests on the heterogeneity of cognitive orientations (natural, legal, social and individual sciences). In his view, the social sciences are distinguishable not because they have spirit as their object rather than nature, or because they incline toward the internal understanding of a phenomenon rather than its causal explanation; what distinguishes them is their particular orientation toward individuality. It is not the object, but the end for which it is examined; thus it is not understanding as immediate intuition but the way in which it arrives at an empirical validification, by translation into a specific form of causal explanation, which makes the social sciences distinct and autonomous.

We have already remarked that Dilthey's position should also be reinterpreted. In fact, Weber does not deny that the social sci-

ences have their own field of enquiry and special procedure. He
simply denies that either of these is sufficient to characterize
their logical structure. What might distinguish the cultural from
the natural sciences is no longer the presence or absence of general concepts, but the different function nomological knowledge dis-
charges in their context. In fact, one might say that the theory of
the ideal type is presented as an attempt to bring out the instrumental function of nomological knowledge in the context of the sciences of culture.

For Weber, the interpretive procedure of sociology, as we have
said, is individualist. That is, it rests on the action of individuals
as "functioning types" who emerge in society. Thus,

> The real empirical sociological investigation begins with the question: What
> motives determine and lead the individual members and participants in this so-
> cialistic community to behave in such a way that the community came into being
> in the first place and that it continues to exist?[36]

This individualistic method, he specifies, does not mean individualistic evaluation, just as the conceptual-rational elaboration of the
ideal type does not involve a belief in the prevalence of rational
motives. By referring concepts concerning collectivity to concrete
human operations, or the action of individuals differentiated in
typical ways, he clearly does not want to destroy human bonds or
links but rather to rediscover their real roots.

The action that is of special interest to "understanding" sociology
is, as Weber terms it, "intelligible on the grounds of its meaning."
It is the attitude referred by the agent to the attitudes of others,
codetermined by this meaningful reference, which can thus be explained intelligibly on the basis of that meaning. For him, action
is Buddhist contemplation and Christian asceticism, linked mean-
ingfully for the actor with internal objects, as much as it is the
economic concern of one dedicated to material goods, tied to external objects and to the financial and economic workings of the market.

By this Weber does not mean that only action that is rational as
regards its ends is intelligible, and that by definition the abnormal
eludes explanation. "Understanding sociology" can also grasp situations and affective states, and their typical consequences for behavior: "The interpretation of a coherent course of conduct is
'subjectively adequate' (or 'adequate on the level of meaning')

insofar as, according to our habitual modes of thought and feeling, its component parts taken in their mutual relation are recognized to constitute a 'typical' complex of meaning,"[37] precisely so as to be able to determine what is "irrational regarding the aim."

The process of understanding in itself leads to no scientifically valid result. Understanding has scientific validity only when the guiding hypotheses that have been formulated establish an empirical basis of confirmation; when, that is, understanding becomes simultaneously a causal explanation. Thus, in Weber's view, the evidence for an explanation does not imply its validity. In other words, the process of understanding is legitimate so long as it does not involve immediate understanding, but rather the formulation of interpretive hypotheses that must be empirically tested. The social sciences, by making use of the process of interpretation, tend to verify causal relationships between individual phenomena. Thus the understanding of the significance of a phenomenon coincides with the determination of the conditions of its occurrence.

The connection between understanding and causal explanation as the basis for research in the social sciences is thus made clear. It allows us to determine the meaning of behavior, or the intended reference of behavior to that of others, and to understand what directs the activity of man in one direction rather than another. "Understanding" sociology, whose object is not human behavior as such, but rather meaningful behavior, does not therefore exclude causal explanation but, on the contrary, necessarily presupposes it.

Weber and Marx

Weber's attitude toward Marx is important for the understanding of the man himself and the meaning of his work. In fact, he sees Marxism as a practical example of ideal-type construction and of confusion between the spheres of "being" and "should be." Historical materialism is considered as above all a historical-evolutionary hypothesis to be tested against experience. It is thus not a Weltanschauung but a working hypothesis, which ought to have empirical value. According to Antoni, Weber "overcame historical materialism the moment he discovered that irrational motives influenced economic activity in what was sometimes a decisive fashion, and recognized that irrational forces, great utopias, suggestions, and intuitions dominated men and moved history."[1]

This, however, is not a simply ideological or reductive "overcoming," of the sort that counterposes system to system. The view of Albert Salomon, who sees Weber as a "bourgeois Marx," seems to me untenable. Weber's position is intended to be more comprehensive than, and not symmetrical with, the Marxist one. Weber takes a position vis-à-vis historical materialism when he rejects the Marxist assumption of a determined direction of conditioning — one that runs from structure to superstructure and has the character of a general interpretation of history. As against the Marxist assumption of an irreversible determination by the economic instance of every other personal or social state, material or immaterial, Weber proposes a three-part division of social phenomena on the basis of their relation with the economy:

Within the total range of social-economic problems, we are now able to distinguish events and constellations of norms, institutions, etc., the economic aspect of which constitutes their primary cultural significance for us. Such are, for example, the phenomena of the stock exchange and the banking world, which, in the main, interest us only in this respect. This will be the case regularly (but not exclusively) when institutions are involved which were deliberately created or used for economic ends. Such objects of our knowledge we may call "economic" events (or institutions, as the case may be). There are other phenomena, for instance, religious ones, which do not interest us, or at least do not primarily interest us with respect to their economic significance but which, however, under certain circumstances do acquire significance in this regard because they have consequences which are of interest from the economic point of view. These we shall call "economically relevant" phenomena. Finally there are phenomena which are not "economic" in our sense and the economic effects of which are of no, or at best slight, interest to us (e.g. the developments of the artistic taste of a period) but which in individual instances are in their turn more or less strongly influenced in certain important aspects by economic factors such as, for instance, the social stratification of the artistically interested public. We shall call these "economically conditioned phenomena." [2]

This three-part view of social "reality" makes clear the breadth of Weber's approach, and the analytical scheme to which this corresponds. On the basis of this approach, Marx's scheme based on the "material" interests of life into which contemporaries must of necessity enter is clearly rejected:

Undoubtedly the selection of the social-economic aspect of cultural life signifies a very definite delimitation of our theme. It will be said that the economic, or as it has been inaccurately called, the "materialistic" point of view, from which culture is here being considered, is "one-sided." This is true and the one-sidedness is intentional. [3]

However, with this clear rejection, there comes also a renewed trust in his own scientific method, which ultimately recognizes the importance of the economic function in the coordinated whole of structures and motivations on which the setup and dynamism of the social process are dependent.

Liberated as we are from the antiquated notion that all cultural phenomena can be deduced as a product or function of the constellation of "material" interests, we believe nevertheless that the analysis of social and cultural phenomena with special reference to their economic ramifications was a scientific principle of creative fruitfulness and, with careful application and freedom from dogmatic restrictions, will remain such for a very long time to come. The so-called "materialistic conception of history" as a Weltanschauung or as a formula for the causal explanation of historical reality is to be rejected most emphatically. The advancement of the economic interpretation of history is one of the most important aims of our journal. [4]

Weber is thus not opposed to seeking an explanation of history in economic terms. What he rejects is the absolutizing petrifaction of this explicative criterion, its solidification into a dogma. In **the** face of this danger, Weber is sharply polemical:

The so-called "materialistic conception of history" with the crude elements of genius of the early form which appeared, for instance, in the Communist Manifesto, still prevails only in the minds of laymen and dilettantes. In these circles one still finds the peculiar condition that their need for a causal explanation of an historical event is never satisfied until somewhere or somehow economic causes are shown (or seem) to be operative. Where this however is the case, they content themselves with the most threadbare hypotheses and the most general phrases since they have then satisfied their dogmatic need to believe that the economic "factor" is the "real" one, the only "true" one, and the one which "in the last instance is everywhere decisive."[5]

Weber is aware that this phenomenon is not unusual.

Almost all the sciences, from philology to biology, have occasionally claimed to be the sources not only of specialized scientific knowledge but of "Weltanschauungen" as well. Under the impression of the profound cultural significance of modern economic transformations and especially of the far-reaching ramifications of the "labor question," the inevitable monistic tendency of every type of thought which is not self-critical naturally follows this path.[6]

The same holds for anthropologists, who strongly believe that " 'in the last analysis' all historical events are results of the interplay of innate 'racial qualities.' "[7] Nonetheless, Weber accuses those who have accepted the economic interpretation of the historical process of an "unparalleled lack of critical sense."

If, following a period of boundless overestimation, the danger now exists that its scientific value will be underestimated, this is the result of the unexampled naïveté with which the economic interpretation of reality was applied as a "universal" canon which explained all cultural phenomena — i.e., all those which are meaningful to us — as, in the last analysis, economically conditioned.[8]

Weber backs this up with precise critical demands, offers substantiated examples, and brings out the most serious ambiguities and unresolved difficulties in economic reductionism. Its logical form does not seem to be unitary; indeed, reference to causal explanation does not seem possible. However:

Wherever the strictly economic explanation encounters difficulties, various devices are available for maintaining its general validity as the decisive causal factor. Sometimes every historical event which is not explicable by the invocation of economic motives is regarded for that very reason as a scientifically insignificant "accident." At others, the definition of "economic" is stretched beyond recognition so that all human interests which are related in any way whatsoever to the use of material means are included in the definition. If it is historically undeniable that different responses occur in two situations which are economically identical — due to political, religious, climatic and countless other noneconomic determinants — then in order to maintain the primacy of the economic all these factors are reduced to historically accidental "conditions" upon which the economic factor operates as a "cause."[9]

There is another common attempt to justify the predominant significance of the economic element in interpreting the constant correlation and succession of individual moments of cultural life in terms of a causal or functional dependence of the latter on the former, or rather, all the remnants on one factor — the economic. When a particular noneconomic institution has historically performed a specific function for economic class interests — for example, where particular religious institutions let themselves be and indeed were used as "black police" — the whole network of institutions is viewed either as being created precisely for this function, or, wholly metaphysically, as directed fundamentally to a tendency derived from the economic element.[10] In Weber's view, the unilateral and exclusive determination of historical processes by economic ones, the state of production and the use of material resources, and especially the determination of the historical action of men by material interests, in no way satisfies more serious scholars. In no field of cultural phenomena nor of economic processes does reduction to economic causation appear exhaustive, or even merely sufficient. Ideas and the various intellectual, artistic, and religious manifestations in general are not simply echoes of economic situations. For Weber they are forces working in history which condition economic development itself, just as in turn they are conditioned by it. The determination of the extent of that reciprocal influence cannot be decided a priori, by speculation. It can only be the object of an investigation that must from time to time take a particular direction.

It is unnecessary nowadays to go into detail to prove to the specialist that this interpretation of the purpose of the economic analysis of culture is in part the expression of a certain historical constellation which turned its scientific interest towards certain economically conditioned cultural problems, and in part the rabid chauvinism of a specialized department of science. It is clear that today it is antiquated at best. The explanation of everything by economic causes alone is never exhaustive in any sense whatsoever in any sphere of cultural phenomena, not even in the "economic" sphere itself. In principle, a banking history of a nation which adduces only economic motives for explanatory purposes is naturally just as unacceptable as an explanation of the Sistine Madonna as a consequence of the social-economic basis of the epoch in which it was created. It is no way more complete than, for instance, the explanation of capitalism by reference to certain shifts in the content of the religious ideas which played a role in the genesis of the capitalistic attitude; nor is it more exhaustive than the explanation of a political structure from its geographical background. In all of these cases, the degree of significance which we are to attribute to economic factors is decided by the class of causes to which we are to impute those specific elements of the phenomenon in question to which we attach significance in given cases and in which we are interested. [11]

Weber's criticism is not purely negative. Historical materialism is rejected as a general conception of history, but it is valued as indicating a specific direction for research. Among Marxists Weber's thesis found its most valuable and suggestive interpreter in György Lukács. Countering the criticisms made of historical materialism's unilateral nature, Lukács emphasizes the dialectical basis of the Marxist view of history as its fundamental characteristic. In a polemic against Engels's positivistic travesty of Marx's thought into a mechanical relation of determination, it is related to Hegelian categories, which are reinterpreted and provided with new meaning. Marxist orthodoxy is no longer defined in a systematic theory, but rather by the rigorous acceptance of, and faithfulness to, the dialectical method. Historical "facts" are not to be studied and explained in their empirical, specific form, as isolated entities. They must rather be placed in the wider framework of the historical process seen as a totality. Historical understanding thus comes to act as a fulcrum, and is identified with this referral of every "fact" to the "global" process. "Dialectics insists on the concrete unity of the whole. Yet although it exposes these appearances for the illusions they are — albeit illusions necessarily engendered by capitalism — in this 'scientific' atmosphere it still gives the impression of being an arbitrary construction,"[12] though there is a concrete, not abstract, dialectical method, not viewed in the sense of undifferentiated identity, but as the "whole," the concrete reality immanent to all its parts and their foundation. Lukács establishes the relationship between Hegelian dialectic and historical materialism in favor of the latter, as the authentic significance of Hegel's insight; and, by reference to the writings of the young Marx, he sets the terms of the "particular objectivity" of

relations between men. Man as "social being" is the subject of the
historical process, and for him history is indeed "the succession
of those processes in which the forms taken by this activity and the
relations of man to himself (to nature, to other men) are over-
thrown."[13]

Thus, to understand a specific moment in the real functioning of
the process, as regards the totality, means establishing its affinity
to a determinate form of objectivity and, in relation to this form,
also to the others that have preceded it and made its development
possible. In the historical process, as it is realized through the
succession of the forms of objectivity, the dialectical structure
in which those "forms" are "relativized" is revealed. The forms
are relativized insofar as they discover their significance in their
connection with totality in such a way that economic "structure" and
politico-ideological "superstructures," to use Engels's terminology, come to coincide and essentially to converge in the composition of a particular historical phase.

While recognizing equally with Weber the element of technical
and procedural rationality in particular reference to modern capitalism, Lukács immediately connects this organizational rationality
with the "reification" of modern life and the "dehumanization" of
economic relations. The price of capitalist rationality is the
"alienated," "atomized" individual, reduced to an object of exchange and deprived of his essence. Thus the complex phenomenon
called "capitalism," rather than being explained in its particular
individual nature by means of empirical investigation of its distinctive characteristics and the historical conditions that made it possible, is related "dialectically" to the self-development of "totality." What Lukács has to establish is the objective transformation
of relations between men which determined capitalism's birth.
However, this transformation is assumed on a global level, specu-
latively, and is not investigated. In that transformation, besides,
Lukács immediately reads the fate of capitalist society itself —
being led by its own contradictions to negate itself dialectically,
to dissolve into a new society beyond exploitation and alienation.
Thus Lukács replaces Weber's reciprocal conditioning of capitalism by the other basic aspects of the modern world with the priority of the economic order. To this are related an essence and
functions of an original kind, an objective, constructive form to
which must be connected ideological constructs, psychological
motivation, both individual and group, and class consciousness, in
which they find their nourishment and ultimate explanation.

Given these premises, the decisively negative judgment Lukács brings to bear on sociology, and Weber in particular, is not surprising.

For Lukács, the birth of sociology as an independent discipline has its methodological starting point in the proposed independence of social from economic questions; this claimed independence is in turn tied to deep structural crises in the bourgeois economy. The very naturalistic bases of the first sociology conceived of as scientia scientiarum have "the function of eliminating, by means of economics, the contradictory nature of social being, and this is the basic critique of the capitalist system."[14]

Sociology's abandonment of the characteristic of "universal science" is related to its link with the concept of progress, which in any case was primarily set up in conformity with the needs of the bourgeoisie and was supposed to lead to an "idealized capitalist society, as though at the summit of human evolution."[15]

Thus, after a short time, "the scientific, especially biological basis, in step with the general political and economic evolution of the bourgeoisie, is converted into a methodology, and an ideology hostile to progress, and one reactionary in many ways."[16] It turns toward specific research, scarcely opening up the major questions of the structure and development of society. Lukác's critique is especially directed toward a fault he regards as particularly that of very rigorously specialized sciences, derived from their responsibilities as conditioned by the division of labor in capitalism itself. This involves

the need which grows spontaneously and never becomes self-aware in bourgeois methodology — that of transferring the decisive problems of social life away from a special discipline, which is not competent to resolve them, to another specialized discipline which in turn and for the same reason declares itself incompetent. This involves, naturally, the decisive questions of social life, as regards which decadent bourgeois society has an increasing interest in preventing their being clearly formulated and ultimately resolved. Social agnosticism as a form of ideological defence of positions with no hope thus comes to have a methodological tool which, unconsciously, is functional. [17]

Moving on to a more specific confutation of sociological theories, Lukács does not manage to break out of the core of materialist doctrine, against which he says that there is (as opposed to "bourgeois ideologies," and beyond "simple, total ignorance" or "gross, pedantic refusal") a "more subtle rejection" being imposed; and "even though distorted," some aspects compatible with their postulates might be accepted. Therefore, as regards Weber's rejection of the primacy of the economic element, Lukács replies with a similar reproof, noting that "historical materialism also admits that there are complicated relations of reciprocal dependence in concrete social reality (as Engels says, economic causes are only determinant in the last instance)."[18] Lukács observes that "the structure of reciprocal dependency, quite acceptable to modern relativism, must not be upheld; this is just a polemical advance against historical materialism. Max Weber's views lead him to attribute to ideological phenomena (religion) an immanent development derived from within: this tendency is continually transformed into the point of view of those for whom these have priority as the cause of the whole process."[19]

After making it clear that the central problem of German sociology was one of transcending historical materialism with its own theoretical notion of the origin and meaning of capitalism, and after dealing with Sombart's and Weber's efforts, Lukács observes that their methodology does not deal with the real economic problems, such as the question of surplus value and exploitation, and "only apparently" grasps the essence of capitalism.

The fact of the separation of the workers from the means of production and the fact of free labor are certainly recognized by Weber and play an important part in his sociology. The decisive characteristics of capitalism are still rationality and calculability.... This idea means necessarily that the economics of capitalism is understood backwards, in that superficial phenomena interpreted simplistically take on the main role as regards the problem of the development of the productive forces. This abstract deformation gives German sociologists the chance of attributing to certain ideological forms, especially law and religion, a decisive importance equal and even superior to that of economics. From this it follows that in an ever-increasing manner analogies replace the method of causal explanation.[20]

However, where Lukács seems to show a radical misunderstanding of sociology as an empirical science, not speculative but conceptually oriented, is the point at which he brands it as "formalist," "subjectivist," and "agnostic," remarking that consequently it "only manages to point to determinate 'types,' to build typologies and make the phenomena themselves part of them." Later he argues:

It is clear that Weber's sociological categories simply reflect the abstractly formulated psychology of the calculating individual in the capitalist system. The concept of "chance" is on the one hand based on Mach's (empirio-critical)

interpretation of the phenomena of nature, and on the other is derived from the
psychological subjectivism of marginalism. It transforms objective formations
and their metamorphoses, and events themselves, into a chaotic network of
"presumptions," confirmed or not, of "expectations" (in the sense of waiting
for...) satisfied or not. And the evolutionary laws are no less than the
"chance," more or less probable, of seeing each time one or other of these
"presumptions" or "expectations" coming about. [21]

For Weber, the subjectivist character is supposed to be expressed, therefore, "with the greatest clarity" in the concept of
law, precisely viewed as "chance," in which "not only is all objective social reality resolved in a subjectivist manner, but these
same social situations come to take on a complexity which is apparently precise, but really extremely confused."[22]   Lukács insists on explaining, very didactically, how German sociologists
cannot manage to understand or indeed to know "Marxist economics, since they place themselves on the terrain of the new subjectivist vulgar economics. Within this polemical attitude, sociology can only be a specialist science, essentially ancillary as
regards history and yet incapable, because of its formalism," of
any historical explanation. Weber's sociology thus leads to a still
greater irrationalization in restricting the field of action to a mere
technical criticism, or looking for "those means that are appro-
priate in view of a specific end" and establishing "the consequences
that the application of the means required would have...besides the
eventual achievement of the desired goal," with the subsequent exclusion of the normative judgment, the object of faith: "the exclusion of value judgments from sociology, and its seeming purifica-
tion from all irrationalist elements, only lead once more to the
derationalization of the historico-social future."[23]
On the same line of understanding the level of research in
Weber's sociology, there is another emphasis which takes its inspiration from a phrase in his Politische Schriften concerning the
impossibility of "scientifically" sustaining practical commitments
because of the different orders of value in the world, which he sees
as in unresolvable conflict. In this regard, Lukács is forced into
an immediate return to the Marxist theory of class struggle.
Lukács says:

Max Weber runs into the problem dealt with in the Communist Manifesto, according to which history is the history of class struggle. However, since he
could not and would not, because of his Weltanschauung, recognize this as a
fact, as he was not inclined to do so, and, since he was not prepared to draw the

logical dialectical consequences from the dialectical structure of social reality, he was forced to take refuge in irrationalism. This shows very clearly how the irrationalism of the imperialist period gave birth to false solutions to problems which were legitimate in themselves, as they were presented by reality itself. That is, reality, with increasing insistence, poses dialectical questions to the ideologues: these, however, are unable to resolve these dialectically, for social, and thence methodological, reasons. Irrationalism is thus the way to avoid the dialectical solution of a dialectical question. This seeming scientific quality, the exclusion from sociology of value judgments, is thus really the highest point so far reached by irrationalism. [24]

The opposition between Weber on one side, and Marx and Lukács on the other, is therefore radical. Weber, though with the aid of a multiplicity of orders of explanation, believes that he cannot and should not achieve a total explanation, while for Lukács, and Marxists in general, there is no other explanatory scheme aside from that which connects every phenomenon with a particular stage or level of development in a direct, unambiguous manner. From the sociological point of view, the inadequacy of historical materialism as a "model" for the explanation of the "spirit" of capitalism is derived from the lack of possibility of explaining the way in which the economic subject places himself in relation to conditions that have in fact changed. In fact, it is not sufficient to presuppose avarice or, even worse, human wickedness to explain how someone who became a capitalist could actually do so. We are always concerned with psychological categories and, so to speak, "spiritual" motives. The rejection of a critique in terms of the content of Marxist theory is what interests economists like Schumpeter and sociologists like Dahrendorf, who draw attention to those real developments of capitalist society that are empirically determinable. It would be better, however, to emphasize the deep methodological differences (conceptual and analytico-instrumental) that separate Weber from Marx and directly influence their view of the destiny of reason in modern society. I have already noted that Weber did not reject Marxism in order to propose another systematic, closed theory as alternative. He opposed the dogmatic claims of a total explanation of history by way of economics. In expressions like "authentic causes," or "ultimate causes," and "in the last analysis," used in relation to economic facts, he saw a naive justification, without any scientific value, and endowed with a metaphysical outlook, political or ideological.

As regards the "causal explanation" of a particular phenomenon, one may put forward the Marxist reference to an immanent "totality" and the absolute, unilaterally "determining" economic element. This can be contrasted with Weber's model of the empirical establishment of "conditioning." This occurs through a process of choice within the multiplicity of the empirically given and its causal relations. One chooses a finite series and specific orientation of relations — which means isolating only one among the many series of relationships. Engels's explanation, accepted by Lukács himself, that economic causes operate only "in the last instance," changes nothing and involves no substantial limitation; on the other hand it represents a clear confirmation of the presence of a metaphysical type of argument arising from a substratum. However, the accusation leveled against Weber by Lukács, that the former was responsible for an immanent emphasis on ideological phenomena which would thus be predominant over the whole process, was unfounded. The reason for this was that, as we have seen, especially in analyzing religious phenomena, Weber was always concerned to proclaim the interdependence and interaction between "world" and "religion," and even accepts the economic "conditioning" for the growth of the latter. The bidirectional conditioning for which Weber argues makes Lukács's criticism of an "idealist and spiritualist interpretation of history" untenable. Weber does not believe in an absolute manner that ideas move the world. The case of capitalism simply offers the example of a possible tendency of conditioning, in whose context, however, Protestantism is not "the cause" but one of the causes of capitalism, or, better, of certain aspects of capitalism.

As we have seen, the theory of "ideal type" itself, though insufficiently clarified, is alien to a preconstituted systematic doctrine and points only to a provisional "criterion of comparison" with merely instrumental functions. It is hypothetical, prior to being empirically established; by contrast, Marx and Marxists traditionally rush to use the deus ex machina of the dialectic and totality to arrive at an explanation of everything "in the last analysis."

At the same time, the ideal type is distinguished from naturalistic presuppositions and metaphysical claims. Far from considering the more general characteristics as "essential," it proposes setting out the "original" nature of each historical phenomenon. To the extent that it applies to historically individual cases (as, for example, modern Western capitalism), its function is to bring out the characteristic elements, the "unique," not the general traits. While starting from a specific analysis of contemporary society, Marx, by contrast, hopes to be able to propose large-scale historico-evolutionary hypotheses which, by reason of their macroscopic character, run the risk of being transformed into "essences" of all society, all possible history, and thus being solidified into eternal dogma.

Weber regards historical materialism as having a relative validity, but only if it is viewed as a sociological law or hypothesis that must be tested at the empirical level. It is a heuristic principle or "ideal type" which, while it is as unilateral as any other point of view that delimits the field of research, may be valid as a conceptual schema or reference point for specific research. Weber's attempt to stress the ideologizing one-sidedness of the Marxist schema is more intense and evident in his studies of the sociology of religion. Here, in fact, reciprocal conditioning achieves a result of special importance. In his analysis of types of religious community — along with conditioning by class situations, ideological interests, and determinate social strata — there is an attempt to grasp the reciprocal and significant influences of the "lived ethic" on the economy. I have no intention here of expounding a detailed analysis of Weber's studies on comparative religion, with which I deal elsewhere. Here, I shall restrict myself to observations of a general methodological sort which are important for setting up sociological analysis. It should first of all be clear, and should be carefully borne in mind, that Weber proposed to carry out his research on the level of historical reconstruction and empirical observation. He wished to study "the conditions and effects of a particular type of social action. The external courses of religious behavior are so diverse that an understanding of this behavior can only be achieved from the viewpoint of the subjective experiences, ideas, and purposes of the individuals concerned — in short, from the viewpoint of the religious behavior's 'meaning' (Sinn)."[25] Moving on to trace the original form of "action religiously or magically motivated," Weber refers back to a "mundane" process, one that is at least relatively rational: "religious or magical behavior or thinking must not be set apart from the range of everyday purposive conduct, particularly since even the ends of the religious and magical actions are predominantly economic.... The person performing the magical act...will instead distinguish between the greater or lesser ordinariness of the phenomena in question."[26]

From the strictly naturalistic or pre-animist notion, there is an abstractive development toward more complex, animistic forms by way of "the notion that certain beings are concealed 'behind' and responsible for the activity of the charismatically endowed natural objects, artifacts, animals, or persons. This is the belief in spirits."[27] "Spirit" is still conceived of initially in an indeterminate manner, being neither soul, demon, nor god, "but something indeterminate, material yet invisible, nonpersonal and yet somehow endowed with volition. By entering into a concrete object, spirit endows the latter with its distinctive power. The spirit may depart from its host or vessel, leaving the latter inoperative and causing the magician's charisma to fail. In other cases, the spirit may diminish into nothingness, or it may enter into another person or thing."[28]

This process of abstraction — for which the demonstration of a specific economic condition as its precondition is problematic — is most advanced "in those societies within which certain persons possess charismatic magical powers that inhere only in those with special qualifications..., the foundation for the oldest of all 'vocations,' that of the professional necromancer." The magician, by contrast to the layman, is "permanently endowed with charisma. Furthermore, he has turned into an 'enterprise' the distinctive subjective condition that notably represents or mediates charisma, namely ecstasy... [which] occurs in a social form, the orgy,... the primordial form of religious association. But the orgy is an occasional activity, whereas the enterprise of the magician is continuous and he is responsible for its operation."[29] It is precisely "on the basis of the experience with the conditions of orgies, and in all likelihood under the influence of his professional practice" that there "evolved the concept of 'soul' as a separate entity present in, behind or near natural objects, even as the human body contains something that leaves it in dream, syncope, ecstasy, or death."[30]

The specific aspect of this evolutionary process is not so much "personality, impersonality, or suprapersonality" of the extrasensory powers, but the fact that, apart from the things and material events that impinge on our senses, other factors acquire more importance "insofar as and because they mean something."

Magic is thus transformed from being a direct action into a symbolic one[31]; at the same time, the idea that all the personal goods of the dead should accompany them in the tomb takes on a decisive economic importance. This idea is gradually watered down, to the point of being reduced to the requirement not to make use of the goods of the deceased, at least for a certain period, or also often of not using their possessions so as not to arouse their envy.

Primitive naturalism thus is submerged in a complex of symbolic actions through the faithful, ritualistic repetition of magical attitudes proven to be effective, and in this magic circle all fields of human activity become involved.

For this reason the greatest contrasts of purely dogmatic views, even within religions that have undergone rationalization, may be tolerated more easily than innovations in symbolism, which threaten the magical efficacy of action or even — and this is the new concept supervening upon symbolism — arouse the anger of a god or an ancestral spirit. Thus, the question whether the sign of the cross should be made with two or three fingers was a basic reason for the schism of the Russian church as late as the seventeenth century. Again, the fear of giving serious affront to two dozen saints by omitting the days sacred to them from the calendar year has hindered the reception of the Gregorian calendar in Russia until today. Among the magicians of the American Indians, faulty singing during ritual dances was immediately punished by the death of the guilty singer, to remove the evil magic or to avert the anger of the god.... The first and fundamental effect of religious views upon the conduct of life and therefore upon economic activity was generally stereotyping. The alteration of any practice which is somehow executed under the protection of supernatural forces may affect the interests of spirits and gods. To the natural uncertainties and resistances facing every innovator, religion thus adds powerful impediments of its own. The sacred is the uniquely unalterable. [32]

As for the gods, Weber holds that at the beginning they are not regarded as "anthropomorphic" beings, but may often represent an unordered mixture of chance creations accidentally preserved by the cult. A pantheon evolves only when "systematic thinking concerning religious practice and the rationalization of life generally, with its increasing demands upon the gods, have reached a certain level, the details of which may differ greatly from case to case. The emergence of a pantheon entails the specialization and characterization of the various gods as well as the allocation of constant attributes and the differentiation of their jurisdictions."[33] These processes of anthropomorphization and establishment of areas of competence, though partly related to the divinities already in being, involve "the tendency to propel ever further the rationalization of the worship of the gods as well as of the very idea of god,"[34] and exercise a direct influence on the specific characteristics of a people's customs and practices of life. As for the reason that one of many kinds of god should have had predominance over the others: while we have insufficient knowledge of the economic situation and historical conditions that have determined the development of individual peoples, Weber does not hesitate to accept the relationship with economic and generally "worldly" conditions, even though only hypothetically.

These may lie in objects of nature that are important to the economy, such as stellar bodies, or in organic processes that the gods and demons possess or influence, evoke or impede: disease, death, birth, fire, drought, rainstorm, and harvest failure. The outstanding economic importance of certain events may enable a particular god to achieve primacy within the pantheon, as for example the primacy of the god of heaven. He may be conceived of primarily as the master of light and warmth, but among groups that raise cattle he is most frequently conceived of as the lord of reproduction. [35]

On the other hand, the gods (especially the celestial ones who are masters of the stars in their course, which, according to ancient belief, fixes earthly laws) become lords and masters of what has or should have precise rules, particularly as regards "the determination of judicial rules and morality." "Yet there is no concerted action, as there is no individual action, without its special god. Indeed, if an association is to be permanently guaranteed, it must have such a god. Whenever an organization is not the personal power base of an individual ruler, but genuinely an association of man, it has need of a god of its own."[36] Even though monopolistic religions have existed and still exist, and "the path to monotheism has been traversed with varying degrees of consistency, ... nowhere — not even during the Reformation — was the existence of spirits and demons permanently eliminated. ... The decisive consideration was and remains: who is deemed to exert the stronger influence on the interests of the individual in his everyday life, the theoretically supreme god or the lower spirits and demons ?"[37]

The relationship between the god and the charismatic magician itself turns on this collusion between spiritual and material. The action of the god through magic formulas becomes, as it were, pressed into the service of man. In place of strictly magical formulas, in terms of a natural evolution toward more perfect forms, more in harmony with material conditions, there develops a cult which is rationalized as an individual "invocation." In this, "such prayer has a purely businesslike, rationalized form that sets forth the achievements of the supplicant in behalf of the god and then claims adequate recompense therefor,"[38] while, however, there comes into view in the characteristic results of the increasingly broad, rational systematization of the conception of god a certain recession of the original, practical and calculating rationalism. As such primitive rationalism recedes, the significance of distinctively religious behavior is sought less and less in the purely external advantages of everyday economic success. Thus, the goal of religious behavior is successively "irrationalized" until finally otherworldly noneconomic goals come to represent what is distinctive in religious behavior. But for this very reason the extraeconomic evolution just described requires as one of its prerequisites the existence of specific personal carriers.[39]

Analogous to the distinction between "cult" and "magic" is the separation of "magician" from "priest," whose characteristic is no longer the restraining of demons by magical means but rather influence on the gods through "veneration" and regular practice of the cult linked to determined norms, places, and times, and referred to specific groups which comprise the priesthood. "There can be no priesthood without a cult, although there may well be a cult without a specialized priesthood,"[40] just as rationalization of metaphysico-religious ideas, and a specifically religious ethic, is lacking where one of these two terms is missing. "The rationalization of religious life was fragmentary or entirely missing wherever the priesthood failed to achieve independent status and power."[41]

Rationalization of individual meanings into a logical system, together with a comprehensive interpretation of the world and of man's place in it, are immediate needs for the spirit when the problem of meaning is posed. At a certain point the process of rationalization implies a crisis of traditionalism and, vice versa, every acute crisis of traditionalism involves a process of rationalization, as whoever shatters tradition through his own action is forced to clarify his attitudes in relation to those from which he has diverged. On the other hand, the development of what is radically novel, and was counterposed to magic, "generally presupposed the operation of one or both of two forces outside the priesthood: prophets, the bearers of metaphysical or religious ethical revelation, and the laity, the nonpriestly devotees of the cult."[42]

The prophet is important as initiator of a major process of rationalization in interpreting the meaning of the world and the attitudes individuals should adopt in its regard. Weber defines the prophet as "a purely individual bearer of charisma, who by virtue of his mission proclaims a religious doctrine or divine commandment."[43] He is always a man with a mission, who feels himself to be in close relation to a supernatural being or order. The prophet's mission is taken on and carried out without the authorization of any human institution — indeed, often in conscious opposition to institutions. The figure of the prophet, differentiated from the wizard and the priest by virtue of his special authoritarian and doctrinaire ethico-social characteristics, through his prophesyings always provides us with "a unified view of the world derived from a consciously integrated meaningful attitude toward life. To the prophet, both the life of man and the world, both social and cosmic events, have a certain systematic and coherent meaning, to which man's conduct must be oriented if it is to bring salvation, and after which it must be patterned in an integrally meaningful manner."[44]

The appearance of a prophet does, however, have immediate social consequences. The fact that prophecy itself implies a rupture with traditionalism means that the relation of the prophet and of his followers with the society in which they emerge is very problematic — especially as regards the religious tradition, but also for the other elements of that society. Furthermore, in the course of its development this community inevitably undergoes internal changes, especially at the point of the passage from the founder to his successors, as prophetic religion is the source of social organization independently of the spontaneous development of the traditional order. In fact, the structure of the unitary "meaning" provided by prophesying — though this can be radically subdivided, and can gather together into a unity motivations that seem logically heterogeneous — in Weber's view always involves an attempt to systematize all the phenomena of life. Insofar as the construct is not primarily dominated by a need for logical coherence, but rather for practical judgments (even if at different levels and with different consequences), it subsequently involves a synthesis of the practical attitude in order to form a way of carrying on life, however this might manifest itself in individual cases. Weber's description and interpretation of the figure and social role of the prophet sound amazingly close to those of the entrepreneur as "dynamic innovator," as outlined by Joseph A. Schumpeter. The prophet, like Schumpeter's entrepreneur, is a factor that contributes to the breaking up of the routine of the status quo. Yet the act of innovation may be self-limiting — consolidating only if the innovation can translate itself into daily practice rather than being a charismatic fact. Prophesying revelation is not enough: it must be translated into institutional form in order to become the very basis of the community. This occurs historically, Weber observes, when "Such a transformation of a personal following into a permanent congregation is the normal process by which the doctrine of the prophets enters into everyday life, as the function of a permanent institution. Consequently, in this kind of situation they endeavor to create a congregation whereby the personal following of the cult will assume the form of a permanent organization and become a community with fixed rights and duties."[45]

The consequences of a prophetic movement on the social plane, however, depend on the means it uses to realize its religious interests. Every form of religion appears, in fact, as linked to the interests and demands of particular social strata, privileged negatively or positively. However, this does not mean, as Weber often warns, that there is an unequivocal correspondence between "stratum" or "class" and religious orientation. The same condition of a stratum or class can create different forms of religiosity, just as the same form of religion can be accepted by different strata and even be the consequence of their cooperation. The clearest example of the possibility of multiple relations is provided by religions of redemption. Aspiration toward redemption, "the content of which will be different depending upon what one wants to be saved from, and what one wants to be saved for,"[46] is characteristic of many religions, especially as regards the notion of god and sin and, further, the moral sphere, and contacts with the world, especially at those points where specifically sacred religious relationships often go together with the "most serious utilitarian expectations." Thus, wealth is promised to the "ritually pure followers of the Eleusinian mysteries," to the Chinese by "exact observance of the official cult" and personal fulfillment of religious duties, to Zoroastrians, to those practicing the lay morality of Buddhism, to the devout Jew, and, in special cases, to the followers of the ascetic branches of Protestantism. The worldly consequence, with its subsequent practical attitude toward life, is well illustrated by Weber in this particular instance of religious evolution. Redemption

is most likely to acquire such a positive orientation to mundane affairs as the result of a conduct of life which is distinctively determined by religion and given coherence by some central meaning or positive goal. In other words, a quest for salvation in any religious group has the strongest chance of exerting practical influences when there has arisen, out of religious motivations, a systematization of practical conduct resulting from an orientation to certain integral values.[47]

This relationship, which is able to condition the conduct of life, and especially economic attitudes, should not, however, be seen as a necessary determinant, but rather as one simple element. In any case, "The influence any religion exerts on the conduct of life, and especially on the conditions of rebirth, varies in accordance with the particular path to salvation which is desired and striven for, and in accordance with the psychological quality of the salvation in question."[48]

Weber notes two principle paths to redemption. The first, especially important, regards redemption as "the accomplishment of the individual himself without any assistance on the part of supernatural powers."[49] In this case, religious practices and purely ritual ceremonies, which are indispensable means for achieving redemption if they are inspired and rigidly maintained as a total regulation of life, would exclude any possibility of reconciliation with a worldly existence that is devoted, in exemplary fashion, to intensive economic gain. Of special importance indeed, above all for defining oriental religions, which are generally ritualistically hypertrophied, is that

in ritualism the psychological condition striven for ultimately leads directly away from rational activity. Virtually all mystery cults have this effect. Thei1 typical intention is the administration of sacramental grace: redemption from guilt is achieved by the sheer sacredness of the manipulation. Like every form of magic, this process has a tendency to become diverted from everyday life, thereby failing to exert any influence upon it.[50]

When, however, the ritual state of mind is restricted to a mere sentimental attachment, discharged as regards the emotional content in the moment of devotion to produce a lower, transitory state, there is a "doubling" which makes possible greater freedom in "worldly" affairs. The rite is then really only a means for influencing action outside the rite, and it is action which really is primary. "Then the works of salvation are primarily social achievements, distinctively different from cultic performances,"[51] deriving from the characterization of the ritualistic sense of religion in terms of the regulation of day-by-day ethics, through which the individual works out his religious destiny through the effective services he renders seen as "symptoms and expressions of an underlying ethical total personality."[52] The religious person who is conscious of realizing the will of god through his personal rational activity in this world (a god who remains inscrutable nonetheless as regards his ultimate meaning, combined with the understanding of the "meaning" of the world, in perfectly rational terms, seen as a unity transcending every factual reality) can demand as confirmation of his state of grace his real confirmation as regards the order of the world. For him then, this "order" becomes a "vocation."

In the conflict between certain elements of the earthly order with religious values, caused by the fact that no traditional body can fully respond to the requirements of a rationalized notion of the meaning of the universe, which thus produces the need for salvation, Weber sees two possible attitudes, both compatible with a logical, rational understanding. These are the ascetic attitude in which earthly things are to some degree controlled and mastered in the interests of the religious ideal, and the mystical attitude in which these same earthly things are radically downgraded and insignificant. Both these positions are lived out in a radical form by only a minority of individuals. The first may be achieved, on the one hand, via "the mystical practice of the rejection of the world," wherein "concentration upon the actual pursuit of salvation may entail a formal withdrawal from the 'world': from social and psychological ties with the family, from the possession of worldly goods, and from political, economic, artistic and erotic activities — in short, from all creaturely interests,"[53] and the formation of a "self-sufficient poverty" in the face of a concentrated activity in search of salvation. On the other hand, "inner-worldly asceticism," as has been noted, may require "participation within the world (or more precisely, within the institutions of the world but in opposition to them) on the basis of the religious individual's piety and his qualifications as the elect instrument of god."[54]

The second position, in which the particular gift of salvation is "a subjective condition of a distinctive kind, the most notable form of which is mystic illumination,"[55] uses a systematic technique, "contemplation." It cuts itself off radically from mundane interests, and so achieves an indifference vis-à-vis the world, either by fleeing from it or by living in it but not being of it; this is "rejection of the world."

Like the stereotyping action of symbolism as regards specific elements of culture, religion as the depository of the sacred, unchangeable nature of a divine imperative works on the whole domain of the worldly order; by means of its absolute and changeless supremacy it checks the intense activity of rationalizing human institutions from law to economics. On the other hand, Weber notes how the breaking of magical norms or stereotypical rites by prophecy may involve radical, acute, or gradual revolutions in the ordering of daily life, and especially the economy, as well.

This may happen either through the dissolution of the "stereotyping" of specific ritual norms, or through the setting up of a "holy consciousness," pliable and to some extent adaptable in different situations to reciprocally influencing relationships. Again, it may operate from within, on the basis of a management of behavior in life that is determinant, showing itself through a radically researched and internalized problematic.

The more a religion of salvation has been systematized and internalized in the direction of an ethic of ultimate ends (Gesinnungsethik), the greater becomes its tension in relation to the world. This tension between religion and the world appears in a less consistent fashion and less as a matter of principle, so long as the religion has a ritualistic or legalistic form. In these earlier stages, religions of salvation generally assume the same forms and exert the same effects as those of magical ethics.[56]

The religious ethic enters into the terrain of the social order at very different depths. In this, not only differences between magical or ritual bonds, and those between different religions matter: 'In this stage, the religion exercises a stereotyping effect on the entire realm of legal institutions and social conventions, in the same way that symbolism stereotypes certain substantive elements of a culture and prescription of magical taboos stereotypes concrete types of relationships to human beings and to goods."[57]

Religious development thus seems relatively autonomous as regards real economic conditions, and at the same time it acts on the development of economic structures through the various attitudes different forms of religion assume toward the world: these may be attitudes of indifference, rejection, or simple acceptance, or of action that transforms in a particular direction. The distinction between a world-rejecting asceticism and a worldly asceticism marks another stand taken by religion as regards economic life, and thus different economic ethics with a sequence of different economic results for the development of various forms of the economy. Weber's work on the sociology of religion abundantly demonstrates his attitude. Different sociocultural contexts should be investigated without a priori hypostatization of any Gestalt or omnicomprehensive totality. In this sense, the contrast between the approaches of Weber and Marx could not be more basic.

The Destiny of Reason

In other works I have dealt extensively with the meaning of sociology. My point is simple: The meaning of physics is humility before the power of nature (as Bacon said, "Natura nonnisi parendo vincitur"). The meaning of sociology is dissatisfaction with the status quo, with the hope of its radical transformation. The destiny of reason is thus central to sociological research — it is its basic concern. However, this destiny can be no more than illuminated, and certainly not resolved, on the basis of a radical critique of the current social situation in order to transcend, and conceptually master, it. So, this critique requires assumptions. Once tradition goes into crisis as a source of formal, basic legitimacy, sociologists start to look for the bases of the new morality. Spencer's spontaneism is certainly insufficient. His society, which he still defines in terms of cooperation, is only the unstable equilibrium resulting from a violent struggle between individual egoisms, a temporary fusion of individual appetites in the competition for the survival of the fittest. The problem should be put in different terms: How does a society live; how is it formed? Where does it find its moral rules, its norms? How does one "invent" a society? This is Durkheim's problem. How can one have a lay society, an efficient social order, based on an organic, not simply mechanical, solidarity, when revelation and the supranatural basis are declining? Durkheim makes a fundamental criticism of Comte's model, because it is too broad, generic, untestable, and, in short, not "positive" enough. Like Comte, on the other hand, he is afraid of the "anarchy" of individual judgment, and its opposition to psychology in the name of the "specificity of the social" — in fact, because he is afraid of the dissolving of social bonds through the fleeting, capricious instability of individual tastes. Comte saw before him the ruins of the old regime. Durkheim saw, every day,

bitterly, the decadence of civility and public morality behind the
pomp and fatuousness of the Third Republic. C. Wright Mills, who
as a good Texan admitted that he knew little about French sociology,
is right all the same when he sees the concept of "anomie" as
Durkheim's most important contribution to contemporary sociological thought. Anomie describes a social situation in which literally
the "laws," the norms of society have collapsed — those points of
collective reference for directing individual and group behavior.
This is the negation of organic, conscious solidarity. According
to Durkheim, human groups, moving from simple, primitive societies toward forms of sociality that are more complex and differentiated, based on social division of labor and its subsequent
functional interdependence, find in mechanical solidarity a different, organic solidarity. This is not only the condition for survival
and progress, or a Hobbesian social contract, but a basic ethical
value. Mechanical solidarity does not depend on choice. It is a
fact of nature, the chance whereby one can be born in one family
or another, in a given culture, in a particular period. Cold and
unyielding, mechanical solidarity, like "the morality of the vil-
lage," is an extraneously imposed control from which one cannot
escape; there are no alternatives. Organic solidarity, on the other
hand, is not nature, but history. It originates from real human
needs and develops on the basis of conscious choices. It is the expression of a common set of values and systems of meaning em-
bodied in the daily life of the group. Anomie is the pathology of
organic solidarity, its withering and finally its disappearance. Human groups continue to live, but their cohesion is only apparent.
They are united as an aggregate, in purely spatial closeness, elbow
to elbow, but they do not feel themselves bound up in a common
destiny; they have no shared values, experienced in common, and
are only a "lonely crowd," in David Riesman's imaginative phrase.
One thinks of Lewis Mumford and his "megalopolis," which becomes a "necropolis," or of Georg Simmel and the whole question
of "intellectualization," the intellectual, "dessicated" quality of
metropolitan life, and also of returning to the antiurban polemic
of the English romantics; the latter lived through the first "industrial revolution" and thus anticipated its human problems with extraordinary clarity, destined to nourish legions of boring imitators.

Here again there is a basic question. The primal misunderstanding of sociology, in fact, is to be found in the postulate that rationality coincides with preciseness, the mathematizing raison of the
Enlightenment. The whole methodological, basic effort of post-

systemic sociology, as I see it, was to try to get away from that misunderstanding. It is true in the first place for Max Weber. He was linked to the great tradition of German historicism, and central to the Methodenstreit, which painfully seeks a mediation between nature and history, an existential, biographical experience, unique and unrepeatable, and a scientific "law" — an explanatory causal or conditional scheme, capable of explaining phenomena and predicting their development by means of their relatively uniform aspects. In the light of this, Weber seems torn by contradictions. The thinker who seems to have placed the neutrality of the scholar on a theoretical plane, via the almost universally misunderstood principle of "value freedom," suffers from the problems and shares in the destiny of Wilhelmine Germany with unusual intensity.

Weber replaces Durkheim's "social fact" with "social action" or even "acting" (Handeln) as the strategic theme of sociological research. This is always individual, fluid, problematic action, in tension, which becomes social indeed insofar as it continuously considers, during its concrete unfolding, the possible reactions of others. The interests of the individual, his assumptions and ideas, are the point of departure. The function of social science, or culture, as he preferred to call it, lies in clarifying for the individual those rational alternatives that lie before him, or connecting the ends desired to the means at his disposal. Industrial society, insofar as it appeared to be based on the relation between means and ends, was seen by him as a basically rational one, formally organized in an impersonal fashion, anonymous, whose function continuously developed through time and was discharged independently of the individual, or the official, to whom it was entrusted. However, Weber was quite aware that this involved a fragile, indeed a formal, rationality. Throughout his life he was obsessed by a question which recurs in all his work, explicitly or implicitly: What if Marx was right? What if the economic structure, on its own or as a basic prius, was the decisive force in social development? What would happen to the "realm of ideas"? What would be the destiny of reason?

This is the profound meaning of the investigation of relations between ethics and the economic world, between religions and productive and distributive systems. This does not involve a petty anti-Marxist polemic, as Lukács seems to think. It is an attempt to test the Marxian hypothesis by concentrating on its unilaterality, its grandiose design of seeing social reality as the meeting point of a multitude of physical, economic, psychological, and ethicocultural factors which interact in a connected and global manner.

However, the more important question, that of the rationality of industrial society, its nature and limits, is still open. It was to be the task of the great demystifiers of the first half of this century to establish its real terms and identify its specific modes of development. The guiding thread is the idea of progress. This binds and unites the sociologists of the "systematic" age. The means for guaranteeing and realizing progress may diverge to the point of mutually contradicting each other, but the end is not to be contested, and it is shared. The diversity of means proposed does not interfere with the conventional notion that a new saturnia aetas may be possible — means such as the rational organization of society, the scientization of political decision, or the idea of justice, which needs to be transformed into a power idea, or the spontaneity of private initiatives, or the translation of scientific interpretation into projects for political struggle and the winning of power. Systematic sociologists, even when they speak of injustice and alienation, still have the nice feeling of being firmly inserted into history, of knowing exactly what one wants and why, and of having no doubts about the final outcome.

On the other hand, what representative sociologists of the first half of this century have in common is the wary attitude of one who has learned not to trust in ideological prophecy and is not burning to put forward proposals and schemes for tomorrow's world; instead, a cautious tendency, shot through with skepticism, to ask oneself what is "behind" a doctrine, and the need to see clearly the practical origin of a theoretical position. Having rejected the idea of putting forward plans for social reconstruction, the sociologists "demystify" and restrict themselves to asking for further investigation. The arrogance of yesteryear is but a memory.

This task of demystification was begun very rigorously by Marx. It has been noted that all Marx's important works express their critical intention in their titles — The Critique of Hegel's Philosophy of Right, the Introduction to the Critique of Political Economy, and so forth. But what is striking and makes us think is the extraordinary continuity of that underground critical current which finds unexpected outlets, infiltrates various areas of thought and obviously contrasting intellectual tendencies, establishes subtle, mysterious links of intellectual complicity — Marx with Veblen, Pareto, Michels, Mannheim, and Marcuse.

Veblen first: The great provoker, sly, allusive; a resourceful writer, in an English that is polysyllabic, Latinizing, and sinuous,

and unexpectedly sometimes dry and withering, as though all the
previous passages had only been patient preparations for an am-
bush. Dos Passos put it well in Big Money — that he wove a long
rope for society to hang itself on. The expansive Marxist hope for
a genuine workers' internationalism beyond national frontiers, and
the rationality of economic behavior, are the myths Veblen meets
head on. With exceptional insight, and much before the professional political observers, Veblen foresaw the breakup of international working class solidarity even before World War I. In his
Imperial Germany and the Industrial Revolution he argued (as
against the optimism of the current Socialist International) that
any exploitation of the "predatory and sporting attitudes" of the
German working masses would easily suffice to bind them to the
bellicose, "barbaric" designs of the small groups that controlled
big finance capital and were at the root of recent European political
adventures. Reading Veblen, and however distant and "anthropolog-
ico-cultural" it may sound, one is forced to remember the spectre
of the choral totalitarianisms of our day with their clever manipulation of "sporting loyalties" among the mass.

More: In the United States of Wilson's "new freedom," of the
twenties, a country that had only recently discovered mass production, a country that contained in its Puritan foundations a cult of
efficiency, this languid son of Norwegian farmers rose up to attack,
indeed with the peasant's concern for detail, the typical "heroes"
of American society, the businessmen, whether captain of industry
or financier — Dreiser's Titan and Fitzgerald's Great Gatsby.
Veblen's attack is more comprehensive and penetrating than Marx's.
It is not limited to structures, but follows its victim to the roots of
his psychological motives. He demonstrates these for the enlightenment of the reader, but without excessive illusions: the erratic
decisions, the almost congenital irrationality, "honorific consumption," and "conspicuous consumption," but primarily the old "barbaric," "predatory" custom of doing business on the backs of
others, either by war or by economic crises (the fluctuations of
that supreme smiling Providence, the market).

Veblen's analysis leads to a black-and-white picture. On the one
hand we have the "engineer," ready to promote technical progress
and able to understand its logic, but without fixed interests which
might lead him to speculate on the scarcity of goods and become a parasitic absentee owner (many of the praises Veblen sings
of the engineer return almost literally, if with less elegance, in
C. P. Snow's contemporary discussion of the scientist in The Two

Cultures and the Scientific Revolution). On the other hand, we have
the negation, and the caricature, of enterprise — not so much the
captain of industry as the mere speculator, the "captain of business," who makes money from the fluctuations and subsequent re-
adjustments (interstitial adjustments) in difficult economic situations and who buys and sells businesses and firms without ever
having set foot in a factory. He is the manipulator of the "neutral
flow" of money, in Georg Simmel's term, through which everything
is reduced to a homogeneous, grey and uniform quantity. In the
solitude of Palo Alto, where he died, Veblen was too disenchanted
to claim to know where we were going. Only silence and the bitter
defense of irony remained.

Veblen's demystification of classical economics has its analogy
in the work of Pareto and Michels on political democracy. Especially in Anglo-Saxon countries, Pareto, after an initial period of
popularity in the thirties (his Trattato di Sociologia, translated and
abridged with the title The Mind and Society, was a best-seller),
had the misfortune to become regarded as a fascist — the theorist
of the use of force in social relations and by definition the critic
of democracies. Those who meddle with popular myths always run
certain risks. The truth is that among sociologists the only one
who can measure up to Pareto is Marx. These are two great "un-
maskers." Obviously, they are different. One is an Italian aristo-
crat, the other a German professor. The first was Voltairian, un-
conventional and naturally iconoclastic, but also an industrial man-
ager, a real organizer and meticulous administrator (one need only
read the letters he sent to the administration of the canton of Vaud
regarding his salary increases as professor of economics at Lau-
sanne). Marx was an Hegelian malgré lui and a revolutionary,
serious but capable of unforgettable sarcasm and biblical outrage.
The common point is provided by the need to clarify the real conditions of relations, breaking through the crust of "ideal superstructures." Reading Pareto one sees clearly the great amusement
he derives when he wittily overturns the progressive, humanitarian
ideals of the enlightened bourgeoisie of his day. Subdividing men's
actions into logical and nonlogical, he shows that the typical activity
of man is the nonlogical, especially when it comes to politics. The
numerous examples of nonlogical social actions Pareto adduced
in the Trattato betray all too clearly his taste for socking liberal-
democratic rationalism. He implicitly seems to say: It is all quite
different from rational choices by the individual, and from the
general progress of humanity guaranteed by the struggle against

illiteracy and by universal suffrage. In every culture and every
period, basically the same taboos and magic, the same personal
abstractions, evidence of the nonlogical tendency in man, exist.
The forms may change, but the basic part remains unchanged.
Ancient divinities like Athena and Janus are replaced by others
such as "Progress" and "Humanity." The hymns to Jupiter become
today's invocations to the people and to democratic institutions.
The magic of the vote and electoral manipulation supplant the magic
of "wax dolls" and "sorcerers' wands." Faith in progress replaces
revealed religion to all effects. Man is not a rational animal. Under the thin film of rationality there slumbers an instinctive, nonlogical being, swinging between the poles of craftiness and force,
alternately fox and lion.

Later, a not unworthy successor to the tradition of the Italian
elitist school (Mosca, Pareto, and if you wish, Machiavelli before
them), Roberto Michels, posed the theory of "the iron law of oligarchic tendencies." Michels writes skillfully, but his "law" is
such only by means of gross approximation. It is more a happily
summarized formulation of organizational phenomena of which he
had direct experience and which could be read in the newspapers
than a law, a well defined and tested working hypothesis. It has
been said that Michels wrote with scissors, that he collected as
evidence newspaper cuttings, anecdotes, and odd or in any way suggestive facts. Certainly, he can be seen as a precursor of Vance
Packard. The success his book Political Parties now enjoys in the
United States, based on his 1912 La sociologia del partito politico
nella democrazia moderna, is not fortuitous. The new fact to note
is that Michels touches on the internal life of organizational structures with an eye for the discrepancy between official ideological
credo and real power and authority relations. The masses are incapable of autonomous, first-person expression. Democracy is
necessarily a regime of organizations, but they are tendentially
oligarchic, antidemocratic. The reply made by the democrats to
this argument is well known: that Michels was looking for democracy within individual organizations, such as the parties and the
unions, which as a whole, not singly and still less in terms of their
internal relations, make up democracy. An organization is an organism with precise ends that must be achieved. The level of its
functionality can be determined on the basis of its ability to realize
its own specific objectives — which can never be democracy as
such. On the contrary, democracy and the democratic order are
the result of interaction — of the competitive interchange and recip-

rocal control among the different individual organizations, such
that no one of them dominates at the expense of the others, and
above all at the expense of the concrete possibility that any one
might achieve domination. According to the defenders of multi-
party competitive democracy, it consists essentially in the possibility, institutionally guaranteed to all citizens, of choosing between
alternative forms of servitude.

In my view, Michels's interest for us lies elsewhere, in the first
glimpses of the question Mannheim and Marcuse were to locate at
the basis of the development — or the involution — of industrial
society and its human significance. This is the question of the relationship between the original guiding function, which is not foreseen and is of necessity unforeseeable, and the standardized requirements of centralized organization, between creativity and efficiency, the intellectual and the bureaucrat. Where is industrial
society going? What is the role, the function of the intellectual
in this kind of society? Is his function still definable, or is the
intellectual simply someone who has not yet found a job?

The technological unemployment, so to speak, of the intellectual
in a society that has resolved, or is resolving, all its problems
gradually, without ever needing to go beyond itself — to counterpose
itself to itself, hypothesizing and presenting radical, qualitative,
global alternatives — is largely an inescapable result. Yet it is
difficult now to believe in an optimistic construct — that this is a
case that calls only for technical retraining, as in the case of
workers who lose their jobs as a result of automation. It is true
that intellectual labor is the last artisan-type work; but one must
ask, with Marcuse, if its disappearance does not represent a dead
loss for human life, its irreversible impoverishment and its reduction to "one-dimensional humanity." This is still Weber's major
problem: the passage from formal to substantial rationality. Industrial society is rational from a formal legal point of view; that
is, it is rational in the sense that, like a machine, it can take account in terms of efficiency, calculation, and prediction of its own
movements, but cannot tell us much about the reasons for the movements themselves. As with the movement of a machine, which in
Heidegger's phrase is but "the everlasting return of the identical,"
the rationality of industrial society does not go beyond the inherent
correctness of its own operations. It has only internal goals, and
cannot escape from "doing for its own sake," just as it cannot pose
objectives outside itself without denying its own logic, without
transcending itself. It is a society that spreads out horizontally,

tolerates no residues, and coopts everything; it is a society without utopia, and thus without opposition. The task of sociology today is to put this society in crisis by means of research directed toward specific, circumscribed human needs. The destiny of reason, or to put it another way, reason's capability of becoming reasonable, depends on the "recapture" of these real needs, needs not inspired by propaganda or pursued and satisfied only on the basis of a canon of honorific waste for purposes of social prestige.

Weber links this question to points of view, the "interests" of the individual. However, where do these points of view or subjective interests find their justification? This is the basic difficulty which underlies Weber's whole project. For instance, Weber classifies the pure types of sovereignty on the basis of the principles on which they are founded. Sovereignty is the "chance" of finding obedience in a human group based on the possession of economic goods, but above all on authority. Power should be seen as "the probability that certain specific commands (or all commands) will be obeyed by a given group of persons. It thus does not include every mode of exercising 'power' or 'influence' over other persons."[1]

In other words, custom and the system of interests cannot form "a sufficiently reliable basis for a given domination. In addition, there is normally a further element, the belief in legitimacy."[2] Every authority seeks legitimacy according to the type of legiti-macy its power claims. Thus a different power structure, and a different form of obedience on the part of the people, is produced. The principles of legitimacy derived from this premise are tradi-tional, rational, and charismatic. But why isolate and select the motive of legitimacy rather than another, by means of which a dif-ferent theory of power could be formulated? Both the criterion of selection and differentiation, and the construction of "utopian," abstractly rational conceptual frameworks are to a large degree arbitrary. Weber confirms these doubts when he argues that the whole question of science can be reduced to the factual thesis that there are "many, indeed countless, practical questions in the dis-cussion of which there seems to be general agreement about the self-evident character of certain goals."[3] Weber's scientific ideal is purely "rational." However, this is not Kantian rationality, morality, but rather a practical one of "adequacy." For him, whatever the rational impulses and suggestions men experience, actions exam-ined on the basis of the criterion of coherence or conformity of means and end, always partake of the rationality of concrete knowledge, and the intelligibility of social action in all its complexity.

The other basic characteristic of science is that involving its problematic nature: 'It is not the 'actual' interconnections of 'things' but the <u>conceptual</u> interconnections of <u>problems</u> which define the scope of the various sciences. A new 'science' emerges where new problems are pursued by new methods and truths are thereby discovered which open up significant new points of view."[4] Science, in Weber's view, must first of all confine itself to expounding the possible points of view whence one may arrive at one's object, to discuss the different paths that can lead to the chosen goal, and weigh the consequences — including the unwanted ones — that of necessity follow from them. Furthermore, it must express a judgment concerning the greater or lesser adequacy of the technical means used to realize the choice made, and propose means in view of the goals and values chosen, thereby committing people to see the facts — especially the embarrassing and "inconvenient" ones.

What is the basis of these limits, and why should science see its own "law" in them? Weber argues that science cannot avoid respecting them. From the moment when its judgment on the appropriateness of the technical relation between ends and means passes over into a value judgment on the choice or the value chosen, it finds itself "embroiled" in "affairs of faith," personal ideals. By restricting itself to detail, it would deny itself.

As has been observed, science should not and cannot pronounce on taking sides as it cannot set up any criterion for accepting or rejecting any stand. Science has nothing to say in this respect because, as Weber repeatedly stresses, choice precedes, rather than follows, scientific work; the mistake most threatening to the objectivity of science is to believe that the taking up of a position follows, and thus that it might be the result of scientific analysis. Furthermore, as regards the correctness of a choice, one cannot refer to science since then indeed it has completed its task. Weber says that there are many gods to whom one can pray. Since the "savior," the "prophet," is not yet here, rather than becoming tenured professors we must wait. In the darkness surrounding us, the only possibility we have is to serve a science that abstains from judging, and rejects the claim of being basic to the construction of a <u>Weltanschauung</u>.

It has been observed that Weber's distinction between judging and knowing, value judgments and science, slips into evasion, if not "neoromantic rhetoric." However, one must acknowledge that it may yet thereby conceal "the most rigorous, effective criticism

of the values of its time, since that abstention from every judgment reveals a deep distaste for the existing dominant beliefs in
the cultural world of his time, and because he devotes to that distinction his most bitter and severe judgment on the switch effected
by his contemporaries between ideology and truth."[5] However, he
does not manage to effect the transition from formal to substantial
rationality. He states that it is not only intellect that is committed
to the attempt to understand the world of experience, but the whole
man, just as the historical world is intelligible only through this
total participation. As against the neo-Kantians, he argues that the
premises of "understanding" are not pure a priori forms, but concrete, determinate interests.

However, the concern to save science from confusion and ultimate failure leads him to believe that the only certainty science
has is that of the "modes," the "formal structures," of its procedure. Thus, at the very instant he affirms its importance for
modern society, Weber voids it. Bureaucratic rationality is essential for satisfying the normal, daily needs of the community.
However, when it is faced with historical crises and extraordinary
needs that can no longer be confronted with the traditional weapons
of simple legality, then there emerges the natural, charismatic
leader who is not an office holder nor the holder of a professional
qualification. This notion of the charismatic leader also marks
the limit of Weber's contribution. It does in fact mean a rejection
of a rationality that is not purely formal in favor of one that makes
the judgment of the community react on the leader's decisions by
way of a kind of social feedback, through which, historically, a
humanization of power emerges. This task cannot be done properly
and discharged positively in terms of bureaucratic rationality,
which reaches its peak in unilateral technocratic decisions, from
the summit to the base. It is certainly one of Weber's great merits
that he saw clearly the problem presented by the bureaucratization
of modern society. To him, this process cannot be arrested, neither does history provide examples of bureaucracies which have
moved towards decomposition independently of the decline of a
civilization as a whole. We can only stem this process by slowing
it down, and we must do this.

It is terrible to think that the world might one day be full of nothing more than
little cog-wheels, little men clinging to little occupations which set bigger ones
in motion.... This bureaucratic travail leads to despair...and the world could
one day see only men of this type: it is in the development of such a state of
affairs that we are already entangled, and the major problem consequently does

not revolve around how it is possible to advance and accelerate it, but the means, on the contrary, by which to oppose this mechanism so as to keep part of humanity from from such a dismemberment of the soul, this absolute domination of a bureaucratic notion of life.[6]

Weber was not able to elaborate on the means he evoked, nor to provide them for us. However, he gave a decisive blow to the traditional viewpoint of the social sciences, which was satisfied with formal, systematic constructs based on one-way relations between active subjects and passive objects. His pessimism regarding the intelligence, and his optimism regarding the will, are still exemplary for today's sociologist.

Postscript

This book had the good fortune to inspire many, particularly polemical, reviews both in Italy and abroad. There emerged a wide debate, wholly spontaneous and not confined to the modest dialogue of specialist reviews. It rapidly overflowed into the columns of the dailies, and managed, in my view, to dust off and explore the basic problems with which contemporary sociological analysis must come to terms. I do not wish to nourish illusions, in myself or in the reader. This is not the place to sum up such a settling of accounts. At any rate, as I am afraid I shall not be able to reply to all the reviewers, I must content myself as far as possible with replying only to those points on which a clarification by the author may seem useful.

This, to begin, is the case as regards the very acute comments of Kurt H. Wolff.[1] Wolff criticized me basically on two matters: for not having dealt exhaustively with Weber the politician, or the politician manqué, and then for not having explicitly considered the value assumptions that constitute the nineteenth-century notion of the European liberal tradition (individual freedom, dignity, the sense of fairness, respect perhaps not for justice as such, but for the rules of the game). Weber, even when speaking of the "polytheism of values," took this for granted and as beyond discussion — as a permanent acquisition of mankind, within whose limits individual choices must necessarily have free play and expression.

This criticism is only partly justified. As regards the first point, I should just make clear that I cannot be held to account for something I never intended to do. This book evaluates, "uses," Weber as an emblematic figure, even as a personalized, polemical intention, but within a group of problems that go beyond the facts of his biography and are in fact more alive for us than for him. The specific political positions adopted by Weber seem to me today

to be devoid of theoretical and practical interest, except retro-
spectively. This is his general, almost obsessive concern: What
will happen to the realm of ideas in a bureaucratized society that
is "disenchanted," and whose soul is "dismembered" and "prole-
tarianized"? We have been accustomed to considering a rational-
positivistic Weber, a Weber as cornerstone for the worked-out
designs of Talcott Parsons. It seemed correct to me to choose a
term like "destiny" — the destiny of reason — to restore the general sense of his wholly unsystematic enquiries. These were open
to the problems of the present (the phrase in der Gegenwart crops
up like a leitmotiv), shot through with intuition, erudite tours de
force, crises and retractions, and in places almost anxious, and
moving. Weber the politician certainly has his importance, and I
shall shortly return to this. The elitist limits of his makeup will
be clarified so as to show the falseness of the dilemma he places
in the path of democratic development, beyond the nineteenth century formulas of a democracy of notables: that is, either democracy led by the Führer or a government by faction, disarticulation
and a fall into the swamp of the camarilla. That Weber should have
seen no way out except by magic, through the charismatic leader
and the divine inspiration he embodies, seems to me a crude, irrationalist residue whose tragic, immanent reality he was not able
to evaluate.

It is only with greater difficulty that I can shake off Wolff's second criticism. This concerns the insufficiently illustrated analysis
of Weber's value assumptions. I recognize that I am impatient and
sometimes tend to treat important thinkers strictly according to
my own aims, without much ceremony and even with an element of
irreverence. Indeed, it has never occurred to me to write a book
in the frame of mind of someone who is writing a dissertation. I
am almost contradictory in my liking for digressions and short-
cuts. Let's call it a chaos with aesthetic justifications. More precisely — and here I think Wolff will agree — I follow an internal
problem, one that dominates and grows day and night into an ob-
session to which I firmly subordinate everything, and for which
everything becomes fuel for the experiment, expendable. A thinker
and philologist of Wolff's refinement, able to follow a thought —
always the same one — patiently and subtly through the undergrowth
of different periods and authors — like the tail of a comet — can
only turn up his nose. However, at the same time he cannot be
unaware that I have a plan, and that Weber, Durkheim, Mannheim,
Parsons, and Marcuse do not in this case stand for themselves,

but rather have their own part to play. Wolff knows and states this, when he argues that the answers I am seeking are to be found in the theoretical, conceptual framework of "sociology as participation"; and for this I am grateful to him. He has seen very clearly what I am looking for, the "substantial reason underlying recognition of human needs insofar as these change historically only within definable limits," within, that is, an "historical horizon."

However, the conclusion, putting me brusquely in the company of Marcuse ("a radical social critique of the Marcusean type"), needs a correction. I have great respect for Herbert Marcuse and for his attempt at an impossible reconciliation (a kind of lay Trinity) of Hegel, Marx, and Freud. Elsewhere I have remarked that the critique against industrial society that Marcuse has been developing for some time, especially in Eros and Civilization, and more recently in One-dimensional Man, contains cues that must not be exhausted and discarded. However, I have always hastened to add that in this critique there is also present the mortal danger of philosophical presumptuousness, which, in order to transcend the empirical given, ends up by neglecting it as useless, an irrelevant stumbling block in the path of the enquiry. This aspect of Marcuse's work, which, after all is its characteristic approach — this urgent, violent hubris which makes it impatient in the face of the tiny details of circumscribed, historically determined experience, the fascinating mixture of swift intelligence and aristocratic distance — has an immediate correspondence with the man himself. Tall, with a youthful complexion, big but not fat, with the still thick, silver hair of a celebrated Middle European conductor, he has an upright, almost solemn stance, strangely bent back like one who always keeps his distance, or like a poplar against the wind.

It is no wonder that with him conversation is difficult, disconnected, like a tête-à-tête with a beautiful woman. Clearly, he is a man who knows how, and wants, to say "no," who explains and subtly defends the liberating power of negative thought; but it would be simplistic, perhaps even ingenuous, to rush into arguing that this concerns only someone with a facility for protest. I am flattered that Wolff should put me with Marcuse, though I must immediately make my position clear. Were he not almost wholly immersed in historicity, and if human experience did provide at least a metahistorical margin, I should see in Marcuse a compatible fellow-traveler of Camus's homme révolté. As it is, he is still, among all modern writers on social matters, the most genuine representative of dialectical impatience: more rigorous than

Adorno, more logical than Horkheimer. It is the paradox of an existence naturally pushed to marginal situations, where the contradictions mature, are aggravated, and explode, that he should thus have chosen (as against the Dioscuri of the Frankfurt school) to carry on living and working in the United States. In the heart of that suburban sadness and pullulating flatness which seem to him the sign of internal American stagnation, in that political and cultural situation, every problem tends to be seen and tackled in a framework of judicious minimalism — scientifically, that is, on the basis of a positive estimate of the means available and their adequacy as regards the ends desired.

The book in which one can most clearly see the reasons for differentiating Marcuse's positions, and that which in my view, allows one to get out of the shallows of abstract, or mystified, dialectical reasoning, is probably Reason and Revolution. This is a passionate defense of Hegel. It is also, in retaliation, an attack (so fierce as to emerge as sophistry) on positivism and on Auguste Comte in particular. The defense of Hegel is difficult, especially for anyone undertaking the elimination of the practical political implications of Hegelian thought, the justification and glorification of Prussian absolutism — an anticipation, more than a little disturbing, of the "ethical State." Above all it is difficult now that the memory and experience of this century's totalitarianisms are still fresh and present. At the biographical level, the defense is impossible. Karl Rosenkranz, the official biographer of Hegel who was commissioned by the widow, himself abstained from getting involved in biographical data and from setting out the caprices and the incredibly shabby animosities of Hegel the academic. This need had already been foreseen by his great contemporary, Schopenhauer (see especially The Philosophy of the Universities).

Sidney Hook has recently come back to this theme, in an essay titled "Hegel's Apologists."[2] To his and other similar demands, however, Marcuse can always propose a simple fin de non recevoir. Indeed, he is dealing with ideas, not biographical curiosities, with theory, not psychology. His basic thesis is quickly expressed. Hegelian dialectical thought, in its genuine interpretation, is a corrosive acid, transcending the pure givenness of experience. It does not stop at empirically revealed facts: it directs one in principle to the totality, to the global meaning, and is thus critical, antidogmatic, and liberating.

The exposition of this thesis is a bravura piece and occupies the whole of the first part of Reason and Revolution.[3] The second part is devoted to the exposition of the perversion of those needs that lie at the basis of Hegelian thought; in other words, the "fall," connected with the confusion between "reason" and "intellect," or between dialectical thought and "abstract scientific," "positivistic" thought, which precedes the rise of "social theory." With the same eagerness with which in the first part he takes care to free Hegel from the reputation of being a "fascist totalitarian," still less a justifier of the Prussian state, Marcuse then tries to establish the conception of Comte as the prophet of reaction and political dogmatism. However, the attempt does not seem to me to go much beyond an interesting collection of quotations cobbled together for polemical reasons, out of context. The overall result is a harsh attack launched against sociology and generally against all the social sciences. The violence of the attack can be seen in Marcuse's language. For example, "Comte begins his propaganda for positivism..." (p. 345). Yet this "propaganda" must be fairly well thought-out if a thinker like Marcuse devotes dozens of pages to it.

These are Marcuse's lines of argument: "Resignation is a basic note in Comte's writings, deriving directly from the acceptance of the principle of the invariability of social laws" (p. 381). This resignation, or submission to the real (the recognition of empirical facts as absolutely fundamental), is opposed to the traditional theological and speculative notions. But Marcuse, echoed in his own way and in various keys by Adorno and disciples, argues that this recognition of the facts, common to positivism and to sociology, as to all modern sciences of nature as well as "culture" (to use the formula Rickert and Weber prefer to Dilthey's "sciences of the spirit"), in reality means digestion, absorption, or annihilation of the facts that are no longer conceptually capable of being mastered. Indeed, "Positivism...gradually substituted for thought understood as free spontaneity, a thought whose functions were predominantly receptive" (p. 343).

The skill with which Marcuse makes his argument, using precisely selected quotations, is undeniable; but his conclusion is untenable. Far from being consumed by elementary facts, Comte never tires of invoking "the clear indication of a preliminary theory... without which the observer would not even know...what he has to examine in the fact appearing before his eyes."[4] Far from wanting to justify, if not install, a totalitarian dictatorship, Comte, in the disturbed postrevolutionary world, was concerned to find a new basis of social consensus; he thought he had identified it in the "scientization" of political judgment, or in a political judgment removed from personal idiosyncrasies, as though from the weight of the dead hand of tradition.

Is it excessive to see in Comte the precursor of the processes of rational socioeconomic planning now in existence, or at least being planned, both in the East and the West? Possibly, though it is hard to deny that even today his importance is linked to a precise, incontestable fact — that he saw with extraordinary acuteness the connection joining science and society. Marx correctly foresaw massive industrialization. Proudhon has the undoubted historical value of having underlined the advantages of federalist political structures. Comte grasped the social importance of science, and described the essential character of industrial society as one based on rational, all-inclusive calculation in which class struggle itself came to be included as part of the pluralistic interplay of interests: an organized and socio-centric society. Above all, he understood that science could no longer be seen as an individual fact, suspended between esoteric practice and witchcraft, but rather as a most powerful instrument of social analysis and transformation. It is strange that on this aspect of Comte's thought Marcuse has nothing to say.

The problems that he raises are by no means phantasms, but his conceptual frame of reference, his perspective, and the general direction of his enquiry do not seem to me to avoid the sorry result of an almost decadent catastrophism. They remain as reminders, danger signals, and pedagogic warnings rather than scientific propositions. Their very suggestiveness in any case places them outside any attempt to verify them empirically in the strict sense. The need for totality, the necessity for a global vision, the withering of human reason into the purely taxonomic faculty of abstract intellect, the dehumanization of science and so forth, are concerns that turn up in different periods and authors, from John Ruskin to Horkheimer (The Eclipse of Reason) and von Hayek (The Counter-revolution of Science). I do not want to set them aside with a gesture of distaste, as has been attempted. They involve real problems, though even with the scientific means now at our disposal we cannot fully express them in operative, verifiable terms.

A piece of evidence like that in Darwin's Autobiography cannot be allowed to pass unnoticed:

My mind seems to have become a kind of machine for grinding general laws out of large collections of facts, but why this should have caused the atrophy of that

part of the brain alone, on which the higher tastes depend, I cannot conceive...
if I had to live my life again, I would have made a rule to read some poetry and
listen to some music at least once every week; for perhaps the parts of my
brain now atrophied would thus have been kept active through use. The loss of
these tastes is a loss of happiness, and may possibly be injurious to the intellect, and more probably to the moral character, by enfeebling the emotional
part of our nature.

I do not know if Marcuse would be pleased were we to use Darwin's words as a comment on and criticism of his theory of "one-
dimensional" man, man so integrated as to appear flattened, so
bonded to the "given," so careful to "accept facts" as to reduce
himself — now distant from really human problems, from the sense
of technically nonresolvable tensions — to a "fact," a thing, a number, a stage in a standardized process whose terms and motivation,
if there are any, escape him and fall outside his control. I should
subscribe to Wolff's definition of me as "Marcusean" had Marcuse
undertaken his own analysis to give more detail and awareness to
the basic contradiction of our times — the pressing reality of the
physical sciences, which have, in the name of objectivity, lost
sight of their human aim; and, at the same time, the humanistic
sciences, which, at the very moment they are entrusted with the
"noble values" and human content, can no longer speak the words
of everyday truth. All the more, too, because I hear in Marcuse
here and there the subterranean murmur of notions and formulations I find in the young, less well-known Hegel, from time to time
mystical and demoniacal, shadowy and prophetic.

Instead, it seems clear to me that in One-dimensional Man
Marcuse, in passages that often indulgently skip from the metaphysical plane to the journalistic-impressionistic or from the
theoretical level to that of the most disconnected and deficient
empirico-descriptive observation, has polemized against positivism — historical, logical, and linguistic — without, however,
offering alternative solutions in the last resort. He acknowledges
the value of positive thought, which puts the principle of authority
in crisis by recalling one to experience and empirical validation
and thus laying the basis, historically, for rational struggle against
obscurantist myths and mystifications. However, he does not go
beyond the untenable conception of positivism as the mere accumulation of fragmentary empirical data. As a good romantic revolutionary, he sniffs out the limit in the fact — in every fact, in the
voice of factual commonsense, in the reasonableness of concrete
things. Above all, he fears that the investigation of the fact might

rise up before thought as an impassable limit. He is afraid that the
analytical datum that has not been transcended, experienced in its
dense "factuality," may lead thought to reject a total perspective,
conceptually capable of dominating the globality of the social process and of connecting human ends to this without suffering their
mechanical logic, without deluding oneself that the ends are already
present, necessarily implicit in the mechanical rules of its function.

I share this concern for totality. The empirical "given" has no
cognitive value; in its isolation, left to itself, it is literally absurd.
It has a value, it "speaks," if placed systematically in relation to
social totality and if it is seen in dialectical relation to the position
of the social system, viewed as a global system of forces that confront each other dialectically and mutually condition each other.
This, after all, is the basic condition that provides social research
with its orientation and saves it from a baseless fragmentation and
manipulatory temptations.

On the contrary, what seems to me unresolved in Marcuse, as
in Adorno and others, concerns the question of the relation between
analytical datum and dialectical synthesis, empirical enquiry and
connection with global society. The theorist's impatience here
leaves us open to grave danger. When, in the Critique de la raison
dialectique, Sartre invokes totalization in order to escape from the
realm of reformist reasonableness, and talks generically about
patron, ouvrier, and so forth, without specifying or bothering to
define the level of skill or the stage of development of ownership
with which we are dealing, he is talking in elemental archetypes and
is expounding nineteenth-century platonism. Totality runs the risk
of being reduced to an empty totality; the synthesis is more willed
than achieved. It remains a verbal game, saved by its literary suggestiveness.

It seems to me that Marcuse does not emerge from this much
better. His bits of empirical backing are often quotations from the
New York Times, or occasional statements by union leaders, in-
dustrialists, and so on. This is too little: it is too fragile an empirical basis to support that imposing theoretical superstructure.
We are still in an essentially idealist, "conceptuological" perspective.

The demand for totality is of pure Hegelo-Marxist origin. Today,
we recognize that this is a major qualification for seeing Marx as
one of the founders (and not the least of them) of sociology. The
synoptic framework of research, characteristic of sociological

analysis, owes much to him. The most acute Marxists — the students of a nonpetrified Marxism, those who do not limit themselves to seeing it as a bloc of propositions solidified into dogma — are well aware of this. It is this awareness that permeates the critical comments on my book by Mario Spinella,[6] Stefano Garroni,[7] Cosimo Pergola,[8] Luciano Vernetti,[9] and Aldo Zanardo.[10] Clearly, their intellectual perspectives are different. However, one element in common seems to me to be the intention of freeing Marxism from the reputation of being a nineteenth-century, metaphysical type of Weltanschauung. They do not, nevertheless, lose sight of the methodological and substantial need for totality, which I see, even in Marx, as being logically closed off for obvious instrumental objective reasons; they propose to interpret this as a relative totality, to avoid confusion. They are naturally in agreement with a total, conclusive, arid knowledge. Yet, to my great satisfaction, Spinella and Garroni in particular emphasize the need for the orientation of sociological research not only, and not so much, as an ethical requirement or a generically human one, but primarily as a basic prerequisite of the cognitive kind, that is, as a methodological requirement.

Certainly some time it will also be necessary to resolve to clarify why Marx is so decisively important for sociological analysis and in what sense there burns in Marxism (especially in the young Marx, but also in Capital) a sociological priority directed toward tackling the social phenomenon globally and in a coordinated manner, so as to relate every specific analysis to the state of the system as such. Merleau-Ponty puts it well:

If we referred not only to Marx's and Engels's formulas but to Marx's work itself, we would see that he set no limit to the immanent study of diplomacy, to the effectiveness of diplomatic action. He spent long days at the British Museum digging through diplomatic manuscripts concerning the Anglo-Russian collaboration of Peter the Great up to the end of the eighteenth century, and devoting a detailed study to them in which economic and social history play only an unobtrusive role.

How could it be otherwise? Marxism did not want to be one of those "points of view," those "conceptions of the world," those "philosophies of history" which order reality about an arbitrarily chosen principle, but the expression of reality — the formulation of a movement of history which animates ideas, literature, morality, philosophy, and politics at the same time as relationships of production. How could it limit its investigation to one sector of reality? How could it help being pluralistic? How could it help finding the same truth everywhere? There is nothing in principle which prevents us from having access to history through several entrances: they all lead to the same road junction.[11]

Merleau-Ponty's eloquence seems for a while to cloud the difficult question of the continuing causal model of historical Marxism, the unresolved problem of the substructure and superstructure, and the material relations of life as a priority element or "factor." And in fact Merleau-Ponty is quick to retrace his steps:

A philosophical, rigorous, and coherent Marxism admits the plurality of causes in history, deciphers the same dialectic in all of them, and integrates "personal conceptions" instead of excluding them. But to the extent it does so, it is transformed into another philosophy which is quite different than vulgar Marxism, and which Marx undoubtedly would not have wished to recognize as his own.

What an odd, unobserved metamorphosis! How could that be? Undoubtedly, language, the instruments of enquiry, the whole of Marx's methodological system are those of his time. They can be criticized as excessively "simplifying" of historical human experience, "unilateral" as regards the plurality of "causes" (which today we know also to be effects), and "prophetic" rather than scientific as regards the area of generalization of historical-evolutionary hypotheses. However, the global, "synoptic" nature of Marxism remains, and it is this attitude toward sociological analysis that still counts.

It is an approach that those sociologists who do not wish to be restricted to the formal working-out of a new scholasticism, mistaking model building for theory and confusing analytical schemes with historical reality, will never be able to do without. In fact, one knows that precision in the measurement of social facts (behavior and institutions) has its price, imposes drastically reductive procedures as regards the variables involved, and puts the decision of a political leader on the same plane as that of an individual buying his particular brand of cigarette. Concrete human experience emerges impoverished from this. The multidimensional, objective richness of the world of material interests, historically determined, tends to be fragmented, mutilated, and "dominated" in the name of some feature believed indeed to be "dominant." At the same time, historical reality is armored, deformed, and crumbled in a series of fragmentary enquiries, in which both technical perfection and the lack of connection with human ends are equally astounding. In other words, reductionism ends up by welcoming naturalism, by inclining, as a tradition, to give up concrete,

specific understanding of human experience, which can only be historical experience, in favor of a need for systematic standardization fated to turn indefinitely around itself.

The Marxist attempt to provide a dynamic, integrated vision of
"civil society" as a global whole of interacting variables, or as
a developing totality of reciprocal, interdependent conditioning, is
highly instructive even today. In the face of the state of extreme
fragmentation in contemporary sociological research, it should be
constantly recalled. This reminder implies, above all for Italian
culture, a task particularly difficult in itself. Here, in fact, perhaps more than elsewhere, Marx's plan has been viewed and expounded in historicist-dialectical terms and according to a basically idealist perspective, which damages its sociologico-experi-
mental composition. In my view, it is not so important in Italian
culture to establish "how theoretical Marxism was born and died"
as to make clear the fact that Marxism remained for so long "theoretical" in the speculative sense. That is, it remained a doctrine,
instead of being proposed and realized — correctly, in my view —
not as a doctrine of the traditional kind (omni-comprehensive,
metaphysical, ideological-personal), but rather as an abstract synthesis of concrete ways of being, as circumscribed empirical research, in which its own method is realized.

In Italy, after being a philosophy for professors, or a "concep-
tology" without empirical controls, Marxism became a "popular
philosophy," a mass political force contradicting Croce's assess-
ment giving socialism up for dead on the basis of a theoretical account of the "death of Marxism" after 1912. However, it directly
related itself to the natioanl-Neapolitan tradition of idealist historicism, and thus paid a heavy tribute to Croce's <u>ferula</u>. Labriola
had a nice saying that "ideas don't fall from the clouds." It is a
fact that research "on the ground" was lacking, that the great demystifying impetus of Marxism remained a kind of "prologue in
heaven," that there was something of an inclination to counterpose
myth to myth, and that when there were empirical studies, these
were largely set aside at the outset — dogmatically instrument-
alized. The hurry to "totalize" has led to empty, wholly verbal
totalizations — in other words, to abstract, mystified syntheses.
From being an instrument and criterion for directing the living
study of historically mature problems, Marxism has become the
pretext for exegetic exercises, the occasion for a flight from reality, masked by philological passion and the talmudic, conceptuological love of glossing for its own sake. Once more there is a

claim to "thinking history" before knowing it in its empirical, circumscribed form.

In these circumstances, it is not surprising that the revolutionary
process itself should suffer grave, unavoidable involutions of a
bureaucratic, "commissar" kind. The Polish sociologist Zygmunt
Bauman said to me some years ago in Warsaw that Stalinism had
not yet found its Newton. Possibly. However, since then it has
been clear that a monstrous degeneration has taken place, and that
the dictatorship of the proletariat has been transformed into dictatorship over the proletariat. In other words, the technical instruments of social transformation of Soviet reality have inverted the
order of priorities: from being a means of rational articulation between desired objectives and available resources they have been
presented as an end, even as an end in themselves, taking on the
paradoxical nature of a basic irrationality covered up by highly rational procedures, which in reality masked an unlimited despotic
power.

From this precise point of view, what Spinella said about the
"struggle against bureaucracy as a system, bureaucratic rationality, and the processes of bureaucratization which to a growing extent involve modern, complex societies," seems to me exceptionally interesting. Here we are very far from simplistic, dichotomous and essentially reactionary visions of a modern world cut
neatly into two squares of black and white, East and West, capitalism and socialism. We are brought summarily face to face with a
tendency that confronts both East and West, though in different ways
from the institutional point of view and that of intellectual orientation. This also rudely reveals the sophistic and purely formal nature of similar manichaean contrasts. The theme is important and
should not be allowed to slip out by the convenient sidedoor of a
discussion abstractly conceived of as a moralistic recipe good for
all contingencies, or as cover for a void of ideas and an irrationalist, brotherly need for an embrassons-nous. Lack of distinction in
theory is only the premise for gratuitous spreading of confusion.
It seems to me today ever more urgent to restore the clarification of positions in their specific terms, together with the intellectual and moral courage to recognize as such the problems that are
truly common, problems that concern the very possibility of the
survival of humanity.

Mario Spinella returned to this subject[12] to adjust, from the
Marxist side, the aim as regards sociological research; this seems
to me to be important. He says he does not feel like contradicting

me when I reproach "contemporary Marxism for the deficiency of its research 'on the ground,' and the too-long-maintained tendency to replace it by convenient definitions of an idealistic nature." After this frank acknowledgment, Spinella passes to the kernel of his argument, trying to demonstrate that "to oppose bureaucratization in capitalist countries, there is no other possibility, in the last analysis, but class struggle, that is, the struggle to reduce and remove the very framework of the process of bureaucratization. In the socialist countries, on the other hand, it is development itself, the internal dynamics of the system, which tends to produce this result."

I shall make two observations: 1) It is indeed the emphasis on the systematic, macrosociological aspect that leads Marxism and the analysis traditionally related to it to leave the whole problem in obscurity. Today this problem is clearly seen to be of basic importance, a problem of motivations and incentives to action at the level of individuals and primary groups. That means that global analysis at the systemic level falls back into a position of naturalistic stagnancy, even of mechanical automatism. 2) There is a tendency to absorb and to reduce the permanent critical function of the intellectual into the project of class struggle — the production and organization of dissent. This naturally involves an uncomfortable function. However, we know historically that without such a function, society runs the risk of a "commissar-type" involution and bureaucratic hypertrophy through the withering of the intellectual function — by way of, and because of, the blocking of the production and circulation of ideas not predicted by organizational schemes or the letter of the rules.

Here, perhaps, the tension between the technician–scientist and the humanist intellectual becomes clear. It is in this perspective that the discussion about the "two cultures" may hope to achieve something more than a debate over terminology or the expression of academic vanity. Marxist analysis tends to collapse one into the other. When Gramsci argues that even the lowest-skilled technical labor could form the basis for the education of the new type of intellectual, he provides us with the essential elements for the new conception of the intellectual as service intellectual, active if not an activist, distrustful of nonmotivated "gratuitous" thought not connected in some way to the "cause." Yet the technician–scientist and the intellectual, whom for convenience we shall call humanist, cannot be equated without doing violence to things as they are and to the profound needs of social development.

It is clear that culture is singular and that what is needed today
is a culture that we can very elliptically describe as "integrated,"
but that this concerns, as always, a concept-boundary, an ideal,
desirable situation, at all events not to be smuggled in, as a position already secured so cheaply as to turn out as a perfect equa-
tion. In fact, the technician—scientist is first of all an expert, a
specialist. The worth and legitimacy of his contribution is founded
on a specialization. He has his <u>Fach</u>, instrumental like the <u>adi-
aphora</u>. In that sense, he is already in the <u>agora</u>, already tied to
the scheme of organization and its logic, nor does he dream of
putting the type of society to which he belongs into crisis. Essentially I do not share his attitude, but I cannot do less than recall a
passage in Nietzsche which, after all the nonsense about the "two
cultures," has at least the merit of originality. He writes, in
<u>Thoughts Out of Season</u>,[13] that the scientist has qualities much to
be appreciated: above all, honesty and a sense of simplicity, if
this is to be more than waffle, and an inability to simulate which
requires a little wit. . . . On the other hand, this honesty is mostly
of little value, and for science too is seldom fertile because it
concerns commonplace things and usually tells the truth only as
regards simple things or <u>in adiaphoris</u>, since in this respect it suits
idleness better to tell the truth than to keep quiet about it. . . . In
the second place, there is an acute grasp of immediate things,
linked with an enormous myopia as regards what is distant and
general. . . . If the scientist wishes to pass from one point which
has already been explored to another, he concentrates all his investigating powers on the latter. He breaks down an image into
many pieces, like someone who uses opera glasses to view the
stage and sees now a head, now a piece of costume, but never a
complete whole. . .hence he never has a strong sense of everything
in general (the scientist is also believed to be daring, but in fact
he is not — he is just like the mule who does not suffer from gid-
diness).

Nietzsche's prejudices are out in the open; in comparison with
those of C. P. Snow, the author of the short work <u>The Two Cultures
and the Scientific Revolution</u>, they have at least the positive quality
of genius. They bring us back, polemically, to a basic truth: the
instrumentality of the scientist's research does not mean that he,
as an individual, has no ear for ethical questions. He may also
suffer from these to the point of internal torment and neurosis —
the Oppenheimer case was sufficient to demonstrate this. More
simply, it means that he deals with an object incapable of meaning-

ful reactions. The technical perfection of his work does not place
him, directly and initially, face to face with the problem of the aims
of the society in which he lives. The case of the intellectual is different. Here, the ethical option does not arise in the face of results already obtained, and does not concern only the good or bad
use of a discovery. It is present from the beginning, determining
the instruments used; it continuously questions the very bases of
the regime and reserves a doubt, a permanent skeptical demand
and a critical questioning as regards the basic legitimacy of any
kind of coexistence. In this sense, it is the antidogma, the grain
of sand able to interrupt the logic of the system, even if this means
coming away crushed by it.

It is unnecessary to say that the question, far from being obvious,
is presented as complex and tortuous, a real experimentum crucis
of the social sciences. For a recent profession of scientistic faith,
it is enough to read Joseph Lopreato's review of this very book.[14]
This empirical sociologist's lack of understanding when faced with
Weber resembles, paradoxically — or perhaps we should say sym-
metrically — that of Carlo Antoni. They attacked Weber because
he did not give us an accurate philology of the Protestant theological texts. Lopreato reproaches him, after Kurt Samuelsson's
critique,[15] for having used Offenbach's defective statistics. It is
like saying that Durkheim's Suicide and concept of anomie have no
value and are totally discounted because Morrato's statistical series and the registers on which Durkheim worked now seem to us to
be unreliable. A more important point escapes the American critic: the methodological design of Weber, in which finally the two
major groups into which sociological studies are traditionally
divided — the "structural," systematic, macrosociological, and the
"relational," sociopsychological, microsociological — meet or
problematically try to link up. After Weber, despite all the uncertainties from which it would be too easy to escape, as did Lopreato,
arguing that these concern only metaphysical fears — German,
even — one can no longer propose research under the rubric substructure versus superstructure, culture versus personality, or institution versus behavior. I understand Lopreato's concern: he wants
to ensure, by way of the divorce between "fact" and "value" (though
facts do not speak of their own accord!), the "scientific" nature of
sociology. He wants it to be clean, neutral — castrated, even —
just as long as it is scientific. For this reason, he sets up the distinction or "fence" between sociology and "social criticism."
There is no argument if this is intended to emphasize the distinc-

tion between the analytical and the therapeutic-committed moment, though only with the basic reservation that the very exposition of empirical data always implies, for the contemporary observer, a movement from the position of distanced observer to that of participant analyst. However, there is complete, total disagreement if by this formula there is a tendency to counterpose sociology as "pure science" to so-called "social criticism."

I gladly leave it to the psychologists and sociologists of science to discover what is hidden by the myth of "pure science"; that is, if it involves only a fear of manual (labor) contamination, determined by the need to have the recognition of a certain "social respectability," or if, on the other hand, it represents an indispensable means of defense and protection against the pressures of other social, professional groups — the equivalent of hieroglyphs for the priests of ancient Egypt. I am anxious only to clarify the danger that such a deficient understanding of sociology, theoretically speaking, may bring about the viewing of the field of sociological studies as a smooth, harmonious reality in which theory and research complement each other beautifully, and empirical data and the analysis of the theoretical social system go along together, and everything disappears into a monodic, unmemorable idyllic atmosphere.

Things are different. In my judgment, every sociological investigation that questions reality concretely, not gratuitously, is properly an act of social criticism, and cannot avoid so being unless it falls into pure, and thus interchangeable, technique. In other words, the decision as to whether sociology is critical analysis, or is made into a new technique of conformism at the expense of the highest bidder, is tested in real — determinate and circumscribed — problems of the historical situation in which, in the broad sense, they are developed. This means that in the United States, where there are seven thousand sociologists, not one has anything new to say about the risings of blacks in Los Angeles, Cleveland, Detroit, and Chicago, that none has predicted these uprisings and real insurrections, and that their "scientific" explanations are not too far from the police ones. All this tells me much more about the state of sociology in that country than all Talcott Parson's or Paul F. Lazarsfeld's books put together.

I know that when expressed in these terms, the discussion of sociology goes beyond the confines of the purely theoretical and involves questions of substance. Mino Vianello seems convinced of this when he says[16] that my argument "can take us very far." Indeed, if the central theme in Weber is that of the rationality of industrial society — and of this there is no doubt — and if, then, Weber's concern for organization theory should be viewed in this light, as many have observed, one basically has to have recourse to a conception of history. Ferrarotti sees this clearly — so much so that he turns his attention to the faith in progress that underlaid the last century's sociology, in order to stress the difference in the starting points of the most sensitive sociologists of this century, from Weber to Michels, and from Mannheim to Marcuse. It is the dilemma of the intellectual in industrial society.... Weber linked the question to the point of view of the individual; but whence can these subjective points of view draw their justification?

The question raised by Vianello repeats that posed to me by Wolff, and which in any case I myself raised for Weber, if only in a footnote, though it probably seemed superfluous to him, both because of his certainty about the values of the liberal tradition and because of his intermittent attachment to the world of Values with a capital "V," typical of Rickert.

In Weber's works there are methodological passages that rather take the edge off the defense of Weber from the charge of "dualism" and "metaphysics of values." For example:

In the empirical social sciences, as we have seen, the possibility of meaningful knowledge of what is essential for us in the infinite richness of events is bound up with the unremitting application of viewpoints of a specifically particularized character, which, in the last analysis, are oriented on the basis of evaluative ideas. These evaluative ideas are for their part empirically discoverable and analyzable as elements of meaningful human conduct, but their validity cannot be deduced from empirical data as such. The "objectivity" of the social sciences depends rather on the fact that the empirical data are always related to those evaluative ideas which alone make them worth knowing and the significance of the empirical data is derived from these evaluative ideas. But these data can never become the foundation for the empirically impossible proof of the validity of the evaluative ideas. The belief which we all have in some form or other, in the meta-empirical validity of ultimate and final values, in which the meaning of our existence is rooted, is not incompatible with the incessant changefulness of the concrete viewpoints, from which empirical reality gets its significance.... The light which emanates from those highest evaluative ideas always falls on an ever changing finite segment of the vast chaotic stream of events, which flows away through time. [17]

Here, the influence of Rickert would seem to be overwhelming, but one must resist the "slashing" temptation to capitalize on such cracks, so as not to be aware of Weber's deep involvement; at the same time it is important not to take the direction of hagiography. In this context, I find very well-founded the observations in the reviews by Gottfried Eisermann,[18] Franco Crespi,[19] Armando

Catemario,[20] and, with special reference to Weber's famous argument on the genesis of capital, Carlo Tasca.[21]

But it is in Aldo Zanardo's remarks that I find once more the thread of my basic argument. Zanardo starts from a radical critique of my formula of "alienation by technology," and brings out in it a supposed decadent, existentialist foundation, finishing up with a generous act of faith in the future of humanity. I share the act of faith, but the linear character of Zanardo's reasoning seems less convincing. I feel like saying "too good to be true." In shortened form, here are the lines of the argument: To talk of industrial society does not mean, today, to talk of human society. However, the dishumanity of industrial society does not involve its structures, rhythms, and ways of development — in a word, its logic. It concerns, rather, its contemporary, transient, forms, its historical formulation; these are not to be hypothesized as the only possible ones. Hence, it is not industrialization as such, but rather an insufficiently extreme form of industrialization, an incomplete one, that may be the source of new forms of alienation.

I do not believe in the thesis whereby inhumanity — the "floating in a void," "doing for its own sake," "mass apathy," and "lack of personal participation" that distinguish modern society — basically derives from industrialization and the modernity of the productive apparatus. Certainly, it is legitimate to leave aside relations of production; and, if many forms of alienation are derived from anachronistic relations of production, others are certainly rooted in a deeper sphere — in industrial reality itself. Nevertheless, I cannot understand exactly what is meant when it is argued that this industrial reality is industrialization tout court, the peak development of the productive forces, rather than a particular form of development of these forces, a particular industrialization, confined to certain countries with particular productive capacities.... In other words, I cannot envisage an alienation tied to industrial production itself, one that cannot be removed thanks to the increase in production and greater productivity by human labor. The sociologist who in his abstract analysis cuts the link that joins his correct analysis to historical totality, in my opinion finds himself exposed to the danger of mistaking for the particular contradictions of modernity or of the affluent society precisely those of nonmodernity or of persisting poverty; and for problems typical of a mythical homo industrialis those typical of an aristocracy or of a historical (American) society, defined and situated in a determinate world. [22]

Zanardo's position is peculiarly close to Marcuse's conclusions. As the latter says in One-dimensional Man, the technological processes of mechanization and standardization could liberate individual energies in a realm of freedom beyond necessity unexplored until now. Though this seems scarcely credible, we are still deal-

ing with the (to me, fatally illusory) idea that there is a homeo-
pathic cure for industrialization, given, of course, that it be taken
in increasingly larger doses. This involves serious efforts; but
they are viewing the problem from the outside. The same misunderstanding colors current observations on "free time," as though
a man who is a slave for most of his days could regain his real
humanity at the factory gates or the office door, by changing his
shirt. The "human recovery" referred to will not be given us by
technique, or by full industrialization. It is only possible by inter-
rupting the technical process from within, at the very moment it
occurs, by humanizing its rhythms and repersonalizing its logic,
even if this means a loss of productivity.

Zanardo and Marcuse, on the other hand, seem to me to be stuck
in the old argument about the use of technique — which can be good
or bad according to the macrosocial ends it serves, independently
of its effective functioning. Marx had already intuited the sophistic
nature of this argument. For Marcuse, it is transformed into a
dythrambic hymn to automation, optical illusions of the mystified
dialectic. What is inevitably the result of a political decision is,
in the last instance, made to appear derived from technical super-
concentration. The instrument that can perfect the repressive,
deeply tyrannical nature of technically advanced societies, and can
indeed, through the rapid elaboration of information and its systematic centralization, supersede the "delegation of authority"
(which in large-scale productive and distributive apparatuses has
been, at least for practical purposes, regarded as necessary), is
transformed by Marcuse into the catalyst of the liberation of humanity. It would allow human beings to conquer the "aesthetic dimension." It is in this dimension that Marcuse sees the two
Freudian principles of reality and pleasure finally reconciled.
The individual once more contains in himself the "higher" and
"lower" human faculties. He is once more an "integral" being;
no more, as in Plato's phrase in the <u>Symposium</u>, like someone
dancing on one leg on a wine skin. However, I do not see how such
human "integration" can, <u>sic et simpliciter,</u> flow out like a gift,
from technique — which has always served precisely to produce
things in the mass and to limit human experiences, thus making
them "functional" and "practical." <u>Timeo Danaos</u> . . . I must also
make a profession of faith: I believe in the future of humanity and
I am ready to pay the price of that belief. In fact, I know that faith
in happiness is seen as vulgar. However, I do fear the gifts of technical progress. I don't know how to imagine them as free and painless.

Marcuse correctly sees in technique a system of dominance at
the structural level. One would need to go deeper and discover
what the flow of production, the "roundabout" of advanced forms
of the production line, the calculating devices in offices, repetition
and boredom, mean for the blue-collar and the white-collar worker. What does it mean to have one's own gestures and movements
mortgaged to the time-and-motion-study department for the next
twenty or thirty years — for a lifetime? Technical progress and
technology in general are organized so as to guarantee the coercive
cohesiveness of the existing system — from the movement of the
apprentice, and from the early morning clock punching. Now Marcuse believes, states, that technique can be adapted for a different
use, on a different organizational basis, and that socialism should
wait for that. But there is only one technique, one scientific organization of labor. Taylorism and Stakhanovism are equal to one
another as regards procedures and even immediate psychological
reflexes. What changes is the destination of the surplus value
produced. The rhythms, the methods, the human factor, in other
words, the relation of domination—submission, or the system of
domination implicit in the spurious collaboration that permits the
technical apparatus to function — these do not change. What
emerges as the decisive element (which I have tried to explain
for years) is not the juridical system, but the planned mechanism,
the modes of effective, specific, daily control, beyond the various
juridical fictions, whereby my life is controlled, "lived" by others.
It is in other hands than my own, it doesn't depend on me and perhaps not even on others as others — that is, as persons — but on
the whole mechanism, the reality-screen, whoever controls and
pulls on the reins of power and sits far away, unknown, unas-
sailable, unmovable, and serene. Deus absconditus!
    Marcuse is thus faced with an alternative he cannot resolve:
either to preserve nothing from repressive society and be regarded
as a Luddite, sentimental and rather archaic, or to accept the instruments that make the world what it is by preventing its transformation. He cannot explain how the world of technique, which is
clearly not all contained in "industrial design," can be reconciled
with the "aesthetic dimension." Need one refer to Freud to be convinced of the impossibility of that reconciliation?
    Finally, Marcuse repeats his hopes for automation. It seems to
him destined to free the individual from needs, from alienated labor, and hence from aggressiveness. And from reason too? In
fact, the world of automation will easily do without reason: art

becomes life, and thought is transformed into action. Once the ends proposed by imagination and fantasy have been attained, once the new age of Saturn has been achieved, and when the problem of the survival and preservation of the human species by means of rational calculation has diminished, reason is smitten by obsolescence and is on the way to technological unemployment. But Marcuse hesitates in the face of a potential distancing of reason from the "aesthetic state." It seems that in the new saturnia aetas, instead of feeding ourselves by hunting and fishing we shall be able to stretch out in the sun with canned meat within reach.

Recently, Marcuse has returned to the problem of the transition from technico-formal rationality to substantial rationality, and in this regard he has tried to redefine the concept of social revolution as a historic moment and the instrument of the major transformation of society as global system. Yet here too there emerges from his arguments a basis that is still romantic and basically static. In fact, Marcuse's vision of one-dimensional society can be persuasively presented and interpreted as the result of an unconscious convergence with the integrationist theses of Parsonian structural-functionalism. The latter does indeed postulate a society wholly concentrated around certain consensual values, deeply internalized by way of different techniques in individuals and groups, to the point of obliterating the capacity to reject, which exists alongside that of adapting, and thus of not being able credibly to explain social change. There is here something very suggestive, if not surprising, in the criticism against the best-known representative of a strictly Hegelian reading of Marx, for a lack of dialectic. However, the charge does not seem to be easily shrugged off. Further, can a totally alienated bureaucratic apparatus be efficient? Can it be efficient to the point of producing, preserving, and self-perpetuating an integrated society, by definition without an opposition? Where will change come from? Or perhaps there is no longer any need even to think about it, in the mood of total, apocalyptic pessimism, which did indeed, until very recently, mark Marcuse's attitude?

Marcuse's reply to these questions does not contain new elements. He has once more evoked protest and confrontation movements now occurring in the world, consisting of marginal groups (third world, blacks, hippies, students, etc.), disparate certainly as regards their social position and motives, but all converging on the "global rejection," the total negation of the system. In fact, from the point of view of Marxism itself, the answer seems particularly weak — for two reasons. First, Marx does not by chance select the working class as the general revolutionary class; he chooses it because it stands in a direct relation to the means of production. Now, what is the position of the marginal groups evoked by Marcuse in relation to the means of production — in relation to the functional needs of the productive structure, the motive power, for Marx, of every society? Second, certainly negation is creative insofar as it does not dilute the contradiction between relations of production and social form, and it pushes the latter toward the liberating explosion; but in Marxist terms, total rejection means putting oneself outside history. Negation is creative on the condition that it present itself as a determinate negation and a specific abstraction.

Only on the basis of these general methodological assumptions is it possible to understand how useless it is to pose the problem of human consciousness, and the possibility of transforming it, in the abstract. Rather than asking the generic unanswerable question "What is man?" one must establish the essential features of the system and the dominant characteristics of which man, historically dated and living, is a derivative function. In this perspective, it is also possible to see that the problem of the individual is not a singular fact.

Explicitly beginning with my interpretation of Weber, Carlo Tullio Altan has put before students of the social sciences a number of intelligent observations.[23] They concern the problem of otherness, and what he calls "the universals of the human condition." From these he derives the concept of "situation," seen as a parameter for testing the functionality of a structure or system. Through this, both on the semantic and the historical and experimental levels, he arrives at an identification of functionality and functioning. With that one certainly cannot say that he has resolved the problem of "What is to be done?"; but we have undoubtedly reached a critical level of discussion in which it is no longer admissible to smuggle in purely tautological propositions. The truth is that faced with the problem of "What is to be done?" we have no exhaustive answers and we cannot trust hurried, doctrinaire formulas. When the all-inclusive nineteenth-century Weltanschauungen have collapsed, it is pointless to try to replace them with swift, superb tours de force by a dialectical intelligence that lacks the instruments for bringing out the empirical data and the everyday quality of human experience, without thus being overcome, and digested, by it. The connection between the macrosociological level of analysis and microsociological, empirical elaboration is not the only basic methodological problem of sociology today. It involves, also, a group of operative possibilities, which, logically, may tend toward the total liberation of man by way of projects directed through social initiative, which can involve him at the level of his immediate experience and connect him with his neighbor — to other men — with the tension of middle-range utopias in which news and history merge and the impulse to a new relational dialectic is born. I know very well that this is not a short-term perspective, one that consoles. I do not, however, count "consolation at all costs" among the many duties of sociology.

Rome, Autumn 1967

Notes

Weber's Intent

1. See, for example, my La sociologia. Storia, concetti, metodi, Turin, 1964, pp. 88-94; and K. Jaspers, Philosophie, Berlin, Springer-Verlag, 1932   (Italian: La mia filosofia, Turin, 1946, especially pp. 91 ff. and 99 ff.; English: Philosophy, Chicago, University of Chicago Press, 1969).

2. A. von Schelting, Max Webers Wissenschaftslehre, Tübingen, 1934; R. Aron, La sociologie allemande contemporaine, Paris, Alcan, 1935 (English: German Sociology, Glencoe, Free Press, 1964), and La philosophie critique de l'histoire, Paris, 1950; P. Rossi, Lo storicismo tedesco contemporaneo, Turin, 1958; and K. Jaspers, Max Weber. Politiker, Forscher, Philosoph, Munich, 1932 (new edition: Munich, 1958) draw attention to the profound unity of Weber's work. See Max Weber, Selections in Translation (ed. by W. G. Runciman), Cambridge, Cambridge University Press, 1978), and especially Economy and Society (ed. by Guenther Roth and Claus Wittich), New York, Bedminster, 1968; The Protestant Ethic and the Spirit of Capitalism, New York, Scribner's, 1958; The Sociology of Religion, Boston, Beacon, 1963; Roscher and Knies: The Logical Problems of Historical Economics, New York, Free Press, 1975 (for original references see Gesammelte Aufsätze zur Wissenschaftslehre, Tübingen, Mohr, 1968).

3. See Marianne Weber, Max Weber. Ein Lebensbild, Heidelberg, 1950.

4. See M. Merleau-Ponty, Les aventures de la dialectique, Paris, 1955 (English: Adventures of the Dialectic, Evanston, Northwestern University Press, 1973, p. 27).

5. See Weber, "Wissenschaft als Beruf," now in Gesammelte

Aufsätze zur Wissenschaftslehre, Tübingen, 1951, pp. 566-97 (English: "Science As a Vocation," in From Max Weber, ed. by H. H. Gerth and C. Wright Mills, New York, Oxford University Press, 1958, p. 150).

6. See in this regard the penetrating remarks of Carlo Antoni, who seems nonetheless to overlook the typically Weberian requirement of a new "vision of life," to be expounded on the basis of results provided by research. In other words, Weber's struggle against metaphysics did not stifle his deep and genuinely metaphysical need for assured values, something that plainly cannot be satisfied by a philistine "metaphysics of the profession," as Antoni argues (C. Antoni, Dallo storicismo alla sociologia, Florence, 1952, p. 144).

7. See, among others, the introduction by E. Sestan to the Italian translation of Die protestantische Ethik und der Geist des Kapitalismus, Rome, 1945; and D. Cantimori, Studi di storia, Turin, 1959, pp. 88-136 (these are three articles previously published in Società: one is the Preface to the Italian translation of "Wissenschaft als Beruf").

8. See W. J. Mommsen, Max Weber und die deutsche Politik, 1890-1920, Tübingen, 1959.

9. See G. Lukács, Karl Marx und Friedrich Engels als Literaturhistoriker, Berlin, Aufbau-Verlag, 1952.

10. See Jaspers, Max Weber, p. 16.

11. See Mommsen, Max Weber, especially "Weltpolitik als Mittel der Behauptung der Nation in der Welt," p. 77 ff., and "Die grosse Alternative: Industrialismus oder Feudalismus," p. 103 ff.

12. K. Jaspers, Philosophische Autobiographie (English: Philosophical Autobiography, New York, Tudor, 1957, p. 57).

13. Lukács, Karl Marx und Friedrich Engels, pp. 163-66.

14. Ibid., p. 165.

15. Lukács; see especially Die Zerstörung der Vernunft, Berlin, Aufbau-Verlag, 1955.

16. See, for one of many examples, the recent D. Henrich, Die Einheit der Wissenschaftslehre Max Webers, Tübingen, 1952, especially the introduction, pp. 1-6, and "Methodenlehre und Philosophie," pp. 103-104.

17. Merleau-Ponty, Adventures, p. 16.

18. The proposed sequence (Dilthey — Rickert — Weber) is concisely set out by H. L. van Breda in the preface to A. Schutz. Collected Papers, I. The Problem of Social Reality, The Hague. 1964, p. ix. Concerning the Rickert–Weber connection, especially in a light

unfavorable to Rickert, Jaspers gives important evidence (in Philosophische Autobiographie, pp. 59-63). Rossi (Lo storicismo, p. 437) is likewise to some extent inclined toward a philosophizing interpretation. Nevertheless, he must be credited with presenting Weber to Italy as a sociologist in a precise sense; see his "La sociologia di Max Weber," Quaderni di Sociologia, 1954, nn. 12-13. Alexander von Schelting suggests (in Die logische Theorie der historischen Wissenschaften von Max Weber und im besonderen sein Begriff des Idealtypus, Tubingen, 1922) that there was a theoretical development of the notions of "possibility" and "reality" in Weber, by way of a comparison with Kant. Antoni argues (Dallo storicismo, p. 179) that "Weber never managed to free himself completely from these philosophical-psychological pretensions." Antoni also proposes a fierce confrontation between "ideal type" and "Platonic idea," which is seriously misleading, insofar as it runs the risk of immediately identifying a methodological argument about concrete sociological investigations with an absolute, metaphysical kind of argument.

19. Jaspers, Max Weber, p. 65.

20. See also Jaspers, Philosophical Autobiography, passim, and his opinion as recorded in E. Baumgarten's introduction to Max Weber, Soziologie, Weltgeschichtliche Analysen, Politik, Stuttgart, 1956, p. xi.

21. Aron tends to view Weber in the perspective of the philosophy of history (German Sociology, p. 67 ff.), while F. Lombardi, with occasional uncertainties, sees him primarily as a sociologist (see especially F. Lombardi, Il piano del nostro sapere, Turin, 1958, pp. 107 and 112-16).

22. See in this regard the penetrating comments of A. Cavalli, "Weber e Sombart e la disputa sui giudizi di valore," in Quaderni di Sociologia; vol. xiii (January-March 1964), especially pp. 35 ff., where, however, Rickert's influence on Weber and his methodology is seen as basic.

23. Jaspers, Philosophical Autobiography, p. 30 ff.

24. This point is made very perceptively by Rossi (Lo storicismo, p. 277).

25. See L. Strauss, Natural Right and History, Chicago, University of Chicago Press, 1953, p. 64.

26. C. Antoni, Dallo storicismo, p. 146.

27. F. De Marchi, "Max Weber," in Humanitas, July 1960, pp. 515-16.

28. Weber, Methodology of the Social Sciences, p. 86.

29. Ibid., p. 87.
30. Ibid., p. 84.
31. Aron, German Sociology, p. 69.
32. Weber, Methodology of the Social Sciences, p. 80.
33. Ibid., p. 80.
34. Ibid., p. 78.
35. Ibid., p. 152.
36. Ibid., p. 72.
37. Ibid., p. 81.
38. Ibid., p. 74.
39. Ibid., p. 72.
40. Ibid., p. 76.
41. In ibid.
42. Ibid., p. 82.
43. See the discussion of Meyer in ibid., p. 145 ff.
44. See ibid.
45. Ibid., p. 84.
46. Aron, German Sociology, p. 71.
47. Weber, Methodology of the Social Sciences, p. 17.
48. Ibid., p. 55.
49. Ibid., p. 18.
50. Ibid., p. 55.
51. Ibid.

Sociological Objectivity

1. Leo Strauss is ironical about what he wittily calls the re-ductio ad Hitlerum: "A view is not refuted by the fact that it happens to have been shared by Hitler" (Strauss, Natural Right, p. 42). However, he also argues that "Weber's thesis necessarily leads to nihilism or to the view that every preference, however evil, base, or insane, has to be judged before the tribunal reason to be as legitimate as any other preference" (Natural Right, p. 42-43).
2. See T. Parsons, The Structure of Social Action, New York, Free Press, 1949.
3. Weber speaks of "value freedom" for the first time in the essay "Der Sinn der 'Wertfreiheit' der soziologischen und ökonomischen Wissenschaften" (1917) (collected in Methodology of the Social Sciences), but he had already used the adjective "value-free" (Wertfrei) in Roscher and Knies.
4. The neonatural-law position of Strauss has generally met with

severe criticisms in Italy. See among others, N. Bobbio: "Unclear
in design, somewhat confused and rhapsodic in its exposition,...
it unleashes a fierce attack against historicism and the ethical doctrine that separates values from facts (which he sees typified in
Max Weber), in order to propose a return to classical natural law,
outside which there is supposed to be nothing but a running toward
the precipice of fanatical obscurantism, nihilism" (Rivista di filosofia, 1954, p. 429). See also G. Fasso: "To mistake historicism
for an ingenuous ethical, empirical relativism either signifies ignorance of the terms of the problem or alternatively is a miser-
able, polemical, dirty trick which one refuses to believe could have
been employed by a scholar such as Strauss" (Il Mulino, 1958,
p. 239).

5. See Weber, Methodology of the Social Sciences, p. 86, ff.

6. For references to this school see Gesammelte Aufsätze zur
Wissenschaftslehre, Tübingen, 1951, pp. 2, 171, 187, 208, 217,
and 385; on the school of "classical political economy" see pp. 7,
8, 30, 31, 32, 39, 41, 104, 115, 118 ff., 130, 131, 188-89, 375 note
87, and 412.

7. The founder of the first school was G. Roscher, and his followers were B. Hildebrand and C. Knies; it must be distinguished
from the "Young Historical School" founded by the historian
Schmoller around 1870. The key figure of the "classical" school
is K. Menger.

8. On the latter see Gesammelte Aufsätze, p. 117 ff., 385, 396,
and 489-540.

9. Weber, Methodology of the Social Sciences, p. 85.

10. Ibid., p. 89.

11. Ibid., p. 98.

12. Ibid., p. 87.

13. Ibid., pp. 85-86.

14. Ibid., p. 87.

15. See especially the essay "The meaning of 'ethical neutrality'
in sociology and economics" (in ibid.), the sections on "value judgments."

16. Ibid., p. 78.

17. Ibid.

18. See Weber's distinction between scientific "explaining"
(erklären: to clarify, the clarity science aims at), and "value"
or "make a value judgment" (werten). What is "valued" or "evaluated" expresses precisely anything in which in some way one
believes, negatively or positively.

19. Ibid., p. 97, ff.
20. Ibid., p. 110.
21. See Weber, Protestant Ethic.
22. In 1921, Honigsheim, who had known Weber well, remarked: "nothing Max Weber had said, done or written was so discussed, commented upon, poorly interpreted, and derided, as his doctrine of value freedom in the science of sociology" (P. Honigsheim, "Max Weber als Soziolog," Kölner Vierteljahreshefte für Sozialwissenschaften, vol. 1, no. 1, 1921, p. 35).
23. The basic problem is unresolved: What is the basis, the source, the "presupposition" of commitment itself. However, as we shall see later, Weber is not interested in this, as these value assumptions or "universal imperatives" he takes for granted.
24. Weber, Methodology of the Social Sciences, p. 104 ff.
25. In this respect the frequent evaluations that "escape" Weber during his analysis are revealing, and have been collected and commented upon, ironically, by Strauss (Natural Right, pp. 54-55).

The Conceptual System

1. Weber, Methodology of the Social Sciences, p. 105.
2. Ibid., p. 105.
3. See Robert K. Merton, Social Theory and Social Structure, Glencoe, Free Press, 1949.
4. See Talcott Parsons, The Structure of Social Action, New York, 1937; The Social System, London, 1952; Structure and Process in Modern Societies, Glencoe, 1960.
5. Weber, Methodology of the Social Sciences, p. 54.
6. Ibid., p. 150.
7. Ibid., p. 157.
8. Ibid., p. 10.
9. Ibid., p. 11.
10. Ibid., p. 12.
11. Ibid., p. 54.
12. Ibid., p. 53.
13. Ibid., p. 53.
14. Ibid., p. 111.
15. Ibid., p. 58.
16. Weber, Essays in Sociology, (ed. by H. H. Gerth and C. Wright Mills), New York, Oxford University Press, 1946, p. 151.
17. Ibid., p. 152.
18. Weber, Methodology of the Social Sciences, p. 13.

19. Ibid., pp. 13-14.
20. Ibid., p. 10.
21. Ibid., p. 12 ff.
22. Ibid., p. 85 ff.

Sociology in Relation to Nature, Biography and History

1. Weber, Economy and Society, vol. 1, p. 4.
2. Ibid., p. 8.
3. Ibid., p. 9.
4. Ibid., p. 22.
5. Ibid., p. 9.
6. Ibid., p. 9.
7. Ibid., p. 19.
8. Ibid., p. 19.
9. Ibid., p. 29.
10. Ibid., p. 9.
11. Ibid., p. 13.
12. Ibid., p. 9.
13. See my article "Methodologia sociologica e ricerce storica," now in La "morte della filosofia" dopo Hegel (Pubblicazione dell'-Istituto di filosofia dell'Università di Roma), Rome, 1958, pp. 91-98.
14. See F. Lombardi, Dopo lo storicismo (Pubblicazione dell' Università di Roma), Rome, 1955, p. 330 ff., in which the various difficulties that the concept of dialectics has presented in the course of the doctrine originated by Hegelian thought are examined. The difficulty mentioned above refers primarily to the so-called "reform of the Hegelian dialectic" proposed in Italy by Giovanni Gentile.
15. Antoni, Lo storicismo, p. 196.
16. See Karl R. Popper, The Poverty of Historicism, London, Routledge and Kegan Paul, 1957.
17. Ibid., p. 76, ff.
18. See W. I. Thomas and F. Znaniecki, The Polish Peasant in Europe and America, New York, 1919, p. 1832 (emphasis in original).
19. See H. Blumer, An Appraisal of Thomas and Znaniecki's "The Polish Peasant in Europe and America," New York, 1939.
20. I made use of this kind of biography in my book (with E. Uccelli and G. Giorgi-Rossi) La piccola città: dati per l'analisi sociologica di una comunità meridionale, Milan, 1959. See also G. W. Allport, The Use of Personal Documents in Psychological

Science, New York, 1942; L. Gottschalk, C. Kluckhorn, R. Angell, The Use of Personal Documents in History, Anthropology and Sociology, New York, 1945; G. A. Lundberg, Social Research, New York, 1929.

21. See H. D. Lasswell, The Political Writings, vol. III, Psychopathology and Politics, Glencoe, Free Press, 1951, p. 9 (emphasis in original).

The Ideal Type

1. See my La sociologia, pp. 91-92.
2. See Weber, Methodology of the Social Sciences, p. 93.
3. Ibid., p. 90.
4. Ibid., p. 54.
5. Ibid., p. 107.
6. Ibid., p. 93.
7. Ibid., p. 90.
8. Ibid., p. 94.
9. Ibid., p. 93.
10. Ibid., p. 90.
11. Ibid., p. 93.
12. Ibid., p. 97.
13. Ibid., p. 172.
14. Ibid., p. 173.
15. Weber, Economy and Society, p. 21.
16. Ibid., p. 20.
17. Weber, Methodology of the Social Sciences, pp. 91-92.
18. Ibid., p. 98.
19. Ibid., p. 90 ff.
20. For "as if," see ibid., p. 171 ff.
21. Ibid., pp. 75-76.
22. For the series of operations leading to causal explanation, see A. von Schelting, Max Webers Wissenschaftslehre, p. 262, and Weber, Methodology of the Social Sciences, p. 76.
23. Ibid., p. 169.
24. Ibid., p. 171 ff.
25. Ibid., p. 173.
26. Ibid., p. 173.
27. Ibid., p. 173-74.
28. One can say that Weber applies to this the "principle of probability calculus" set out in a juridical context by von Knies (see his key work, Prinzipien der Wahrscheinlichkeitsrechnung, Frei-

burg, 1886); this is the same as the "ideal ultimate case," in the same sense that it is the "judgment of objective possibility."
29. See Weber, Methodology of the Social Sciences.
30. Weber, Protestant Ethic, p. 27. It should be noted that Weber in a law speaks of "conditions," not "causes." Causes are hidden in the specific concrete phenomenon being analyzed. However, both in the formulation of the law and in its testing through the causal imputation of a specific concrete phenomenon, one always uses "ideal-typical concepts."
31. Weber, Economy and Society, p. 13.
32. Ibid., p. 15.
33. Rossi, Lo storicismo, p. 287.
34. Weber, Economy and Society, p. 9.
35. Ibid., p. 15.
36. Ibid., p. 18.
37. Ibid., p. 11.

Weber and Marx

1. Antoni, Dallo storicismo, p. 127.
2. Weber, Methodology of the Social Sciences, pp. 64-65.
3. Ibid., p. 67.
4. Ibid., p. 68. The review referred to was the Archiv für Sozialwissenschaft und Sozialpolitik, of which Weber was coeditor.
5. Ibid., p. 68-69.
6. Ibid., p. 69.
7. Ibid.
8. Ibid., p. 69-70.
9. Ibid., p. 70.
10. Ibid.
11. Ibid., p. 70-71.
12. Lukács, History and Class Consciousness, p. 6.
13. Ibid., p. 186.
14. Lukács, Die Zerstörung der Vernunft (Italian: La distruzione della ragione, Turin, 1959, p. 591).
15. Ibid.
16. Ibid., pp. 591-92.
17. Ibid.
18. Ibid., p. 610.
19. Ibid., p. 611. See also Lukács, "M. Weber et la sociologie allemande," in La nouvelle critique, vol. vii, no. 67, 1955, p. 78.
20. Lukács, La distruzione, p. 613-14, and "M. Weber," p. 81.

21. Lukács, "M. Weber," p. 86 (emphasis in original).
22. Ibid., p. 86.
23. Lukács, La distruzione, p. 621.
24. Ibid., p. 622.
25. Weber, Economy and Society, vol. 2, p. 399.
26. Ibid., p. 400.
27. Ibid.
28. Ibid.
29. Ibid.
30. Ibid., p. 402.
31. Ibid., p. 403.
32. Ibid., p. 405-6.
33. Ibid., p. 407.
34. Ibid., p. 409.
35. Ibid., p. 409-10.
36. Ibid., p. 411.
37. Ibid., p. 415-16.
38. Ibid., p. 423.
39. Ibid., p. 424.
40. Ibid., p. 426.
41. Ibid.
42. Ibid., p. 427.
43. Ibid., p. 439.
44. Ibid., p. 450.
45. Ibid., p. 454.
46. Ibid., p. 526.
47. Ibid., p. 528.
48. Ibid., p. 529.
49. Ibid., p. 530.
50. Ibid., p. 531.
51. Ibid., p. 532.
52. Ibid., p. 533.
53. Ibid., p. 542.
54. Ibid., p. 542.
55. Ibid., p. 544.
56. Ibid., p. 576-77.
57. Ibid., p. 577.

The Destiny of Reason

1. Weber, Economy and Society, p. 212.
2. Ibid., p. 213.

3. Weber, Methodology of the Social Sciences, p. 55.
4. Ibid., p. 68.
5. A. Villani, L'oggettività delle scienze sociali nella problem-
atica di Max Weber, Milan, 1957, p. 36.
6. From Max Weber's speech at the assembly of the Verein für
Sozialpolitik, 1909.

Postscript

1. Social Research, vol. xxxii, no. 4 (Winter 1965), pp. 487-90.
2. Encounter, May 1966, pp. 84-91.
3. We cite Reason and Revolution, New York, Humanities, 1954.
4. Cours de philosophie positive (English edition: The Positive
Philosophy of Auguste Comte, London, Bell, 1896).
5. We cite The Autobiography of Charles Darwin, New York
Dover, 1958, p. 54.
6. Rinascita, April 10, 1965, and June 5, 1965.
7. L'Unità, May 4, 1965.
8. Mondo operaio, April 1965.
9. La critica sociale, May 5, 1965.
10. L'Unità, July 7, 1965.
11. M. Merleau-Ponty, Signes, Paris, Editions Gallimard, 1960
(English edition: Signs, Evanston, Ill., Northwestern University
Press, 1964, pp. 274-75).
12. Rinascita, June 5, 1965.
13. Thoughts Out of Season (Nietzsche, Werke), Berlin and New
York, Walter de Gruyter, 1972.
14. American Sociological Review, vol. xxxi, no. 5 (October
1966), pp. 721-22.
15. Religion and Economic Action, New York, 1961.
16. Studi di Sociologia, vol. iii, no. 3 (July–September, 1965),
pp. 254-59.
17. Max Weber, Methodology of the Social Sciences, p. 111.
18. Kölner Zeitschrift für Soziologie und Sozialpsychologie, vol.
xvii, no. 3 (October 1966), pp. 562-63.
19. Rivista di Sociologia, vol. iii, no. 6 (January–April 1965),
pp. 155-59.
20. L'Industria, no. 3, 1965, pp. 417-23.
21. Il Popolo, May 4, 1965, p. 3.
22. L'Unità, July 7, 1965, p. 6.
23. C. Tullio Altan, "Srumentalismo, e funzialismo critico in
antropologia culturale," La critica sociologica, no. 1-2, 1967.

About the Author

FRANCO FERRAROTTI is professor of sociology and chairman of the Institute of Sociology at the University of Rome, and editor of the journal La Critica Sociologica. He was an independent member of the Italian Parliament from 1958 to 1963, and then returned to full-time scholarly activity in 1964 as a fellow at the Center for Advanced Studies in the Behavioral Sciences in Palo Alto, California. He has held guest appointments at Columbia University, Boston University, and the City University of New York Graduate Center, and a directorship of studies at the Ecole des Hautes Etudes en Sciences Sociales in Paris. Ferrarotti is a prolific writer in the fields of industrial and urban sociology and social theory. His publications in English include Toward the Social Production of the Sacred (1977), An Alternative Sociology (1979), and articles in Social Research, Social Praxis, and Praxis International. The translator of the present work, JOHN FRASER, currently a visiting professor at the University of Rome, is associate professor of political science at the University of Waterloo in Canada.